The Scanlon Plan . . .

Edited by

FREDERICK G. LESIEUR

The Scanlon Plan . . .

*A Frontier in Labor-
Management Cooperation*

A PUBLICATION OF THE INDUSTRIAL RELATIONS SECTION
MASSACHUSETTS INSTITUTE
OF TECHNOLOGY

The M.I.T. Press
Massachusetts Institute of Technology
Cambridge, Massachusetts

MIT Press

0262620081

**LESIEUR
SCANLON PLAN**

Twelfth printing, 1984

Copyright © 1958

by

The Massachusetts Institute of Technology . . . . .

ISBN 0 262 12003 8 (hardcover)

ISBN 0 262 62008 1 (paperback)

Library of Congress Catalog Card Number: 58-13463

Printed in the United States of America

Foreword

In 1946 Joseph N. Scanlon joined the staff of the Industrial Relations Section, to bring to M.I.T. students his wealth of experience in the labor movement as steelworker, local-union president, close associate of Philip Murray and Clinton Golden, and Research and Engineering Director of the United Steelworkers of America (then affiliated with the C.I.O.). In this latter capacity, he had pioneered in developing union-management cooperation plans in the steel industry, and the Industrial Relations Section sought to draw upon his experience here, too.

What both at first anticipated would be a temporary association became more permanent as Joe Scanlon continued on our staff until his untimely death in January, 1956. In his ten years here, Joe won the hearts of his associates by his warmth, humor, and unselfishness and brought world-wide fame to the Section by his work with management and labor in what came to be universally known as the Scanlon Plan.

When Joe Scanlon died, there were skeptics who said that the Scanlon Plan was so much a part of Joe himself that it could not survive him. None of us believed this at M.I.T., for we recognized the unique character of the ideas Joe developed, and we saw how labor and management changed under their impact. We saw, too, how experience with the Plan developed a man like Frederick G. Lesieur, who came from the shop and was local-union president at Lapointe Machine Tool Company, where the Scanlon Plan has had its longest and most successful history. Lesieur left Lapointe in 1950 to work full time as Joe Scanlon's associate in handling the increasing demands for assistance in introducing the Plan's concepts all over the country. After Joe's death, we asked Fred Lesieur to join our staff and direct the work which Joe had begun. His experience over the past two and a half years shows clearly that the Scanlon Plan has had the vitality to survive the death of its originator.

During five of the ten years Joe Scanlon was with us, he led an annual conference for managements and unions operating under the Plan and for those who were seriously contemplating it. There was no conference in 1955 or 1956 because of his illness and subsequent death. But in May, 1957, under the able direction of Fred Lesieur, we held our largest and most successful Scanlon Plan conference. Nearly 200 management and union officials from 18 companies with the Plan and 13 companies considering its adoption joined with other invited guests in three days of notable addresses and workshop discussions.

Some of the essays in this volume are drawn from talks presented at the 1957 Conference. Others are previously published articles on the Scanlon Plan, and the first three essays in the "Evaluation" section have been especially written for this book.

Two talks at the 1957 Conference by Clinton S. Golden and Douglas McGregor tell the kind of man Joe Scanlon was. Clint Golden, close friend and mentor of Scanlon, was formerly Vice President of the United Steelworkers of America, Labor Director of the European Recovery Program which administered the Marshall Plan, head of the Trade Union Fellowship Program at Harvard, and now consultant to the Ford Foundation. He spoke at every one of our Scanlon Plan conferences, but his 1957 talks capture the essence of Joe's personality and contribution. Douglas McGregor was responsible for bringing Joe Scanlon to M.I.T. in 1946 and has long been a penetrating analyst of the significance of the type of labor-management cooperation provided by the Scanlon Plan.

In the section on the Plan itself, the *Fortune* article by Russell W. Davenport, on the Lapointe Machine Tool Company experience, gives the reader who is unfamiliar with the Scanlon Plan a concise picture of how it works. This is followed by Fred Lesieur's description of "What the Plan Isn't and What It Is," based on his opening informal discussion at the 1957 Conference. The next paper, reprinted from *Personnel*, is by George P. Shultz, now Professor of Industrial

Relations at the University of Chicago School of Business, student and later close associate of Joe Scanlon at M.I.T. for many years. "Measuring Performance Under the Plan" was especially written for this volume by Elbridge S. Puckett, who has worked with both Scanlon and Lesieur as a graduate student and research associate. He analyzes the problem of determining the "ratio"—which is one of the key factors in the Plan. Finally, this section concludes with brief summaries of problems under the Plan, as discussed at the four "workshops" for top management, union officials, personnel directors, and accountants during the 1957 Conference.

The final section on "Evaluation" contains the three new papers prepared for this volume by McGregor, Shultz, and Puckett, together with Clinton Golden's second talk to the 1957 Conference. McGregor's essay considers the psychological significance of the Plan; Shultz analyzes the different environments in which the Plan operates and gives an answer to the often-heard criticism that the Plan will work only under conditions of economic adversity; and Puckett reports on productivity achievements in several companies which he has studied with the assistance of a Ford Foundation Fellowship.

The Appendixes include a Sample Memorandum of Understanding between management and labor in introducing the Plan, together with examples of suggestions which have been made in actual production committee meetings. An early paper by Joe Scanlon, and one of the few he ever wrote, is also included, as are talks at the 1951 annual meeting of the Industrial Relations Research Association by Fred Lesieur and by Robert C. Tait, President of the Stromberg-Carlson Company, where the Plan has been in operation for a number of years.

We in the Industrial Relations Section believe that the addresses and papers in this book will be of wide interest to management and labor in this country and abroad, as well as to students of labor-management relations everywhere. The Scanlon Plan is in successful operation in only a relatively small number of companies and unions, largely because it requires a willingness on their part to experiment and to venture into a new and challenging kind of relationship. Perhaps these papers will suggest to other managements and unions how the Scanlon Plan can open up a whole new area of cooperative labor-management relationships in a democratic and dynamic society.

CHARLES A. MYERS, *Director*
Industrial Relations Section

August, 1958

Acknowledgments

I should like to acknowledge the enormous debt to the many people who have made this book possible. Although I cannot mention by name all of the company and union officials who have made the Scanlon Plan an important part of their way of life and who have participated in the Scanlon Plan Conferences, my debt is probably greatest to them. My deepest gratitude also goes to the contributors who have given us the fruits of their wide experience in the field of labor-management relations.

I wish to express my thanks also to my colleagues in the Industrial Relations Section of M.I.T. for their many constructive comments on the manuscript; to Beatrice A. Rogers of the Industrial Relations Section, who bore the brunt of seeing the manuscript through the press and prepared the index; and to Marjorie Gilbert, Rhoda Abrams, and Ellen Anderson, who helped type the manuscript for publication.

FRED G. LESIEUR
Editor

September, 1958

Contents

PART ONE . . . .

Joe Scanlon:
The Man

CLINTON S. GOLDEN

1 . . . .

A Tribute to Joseph N. Scanlon

Although there have been others who have pioneered in developing constructive union-management relations to a point that made possible some measure of participation in the production processes by the workers, none to my knowledge, achieved the measure of success and recognition that came to Joe Scanlon. Aided and encouraged by the faculty and his associates here at M.I.T., his work constitutes, in my judgment, perhaps the most significant contribution to better union-management relations that has been made in the course of the past two decades.

We live in an age of advancing technology. We are accustomed to hearing daily about new technological developments in the industrial arts, in production, and indeed in the newer so-called service industries. Somehow we seldom hear or even think of a new technology in human and union-management relations. I suggest that Joe Scanlon contributed to, if he did not actually help to create, a technology of participation that has given a new dimension to concepts of union-management relations.

Even superficial observers who have visited companies having the Scanlon Plan in operation have quickly detected the contrast between

2

the climate of relationships and the attitudes of both employees and management there and in other companies having what are generally considered good relations.

Joe Scanlon was not a promoter nor did he seek publicity for the success of his efforts. He was quite content to let his efforts and achievements speak for themselves and to let others learn of his efforts by word of mouth and through the power of example. Nevertheless as his accomplishments became known, they were widely publicized.

Today his work is internationally known. The companies that have profited by the application of his ideas have become enthusiastic proponents of his plan. To the employees of these companies, the monetary rewards that have accrued as a result of their participation are important, but the new and friendlier climate of relations that has resulted is of even greater significance.

It was my good fortune to have known and worked with Joe Scanlon for twenty years prior to his untimely death a little more than a year ago. He was one of the millions who suffered cruelly as a result of the depression of the Thirties. He did not become embittered as a result of these trying experiences. Indeed, while unemployed and without enough food and fuel for his family, he took the leadership among the workers in his community in securing unused land, in borrowing tractors and other equipment, in literally begging seed and fertilizer so that he and his fellow workers could raise food and get wood for fuel to meet their basic needs.

Perhaps it was out of these experiences in cooperative effort to assure simple survival that he first became aware of the capacity of people to work together. As the depression lifted and he was able to get back to work in the local mill, the friendships created in the common struggle for survival encouraged a continuation of cooperative endeavor.

Even before the Steel Workers' Organizing Committee was formed in 1936 and the organizing campaign was launched, a local union had been formed among the employees of the company he worked for. Wages were low, employment was uncertain, and competition for a share in the limited market was keen.

The company had but recently emerged from bankruptcy, equipment was obsolete, and costs were high. Then came the union demands for higher wages and improved conditions of employment to compound the difficulties of management. If the demands were granted, it would threaten the survival of the company.

Joe took the leadership again in this period of adversity. He induced the president of the company to come with a committee of the union employees to the Pittsburgh office of the International Union to seek advice and help if possible. It was at this point my acquaintance with him began.

I have told the story of subsequent events so many times I am reluctant to repeat it. Suffice it to say that I suggested that the group return to the mill and arrange to interview every employee in an effort to enlist his aid and familiarity with work processes in eliminating waste, improving efficiency, reducing cost, and improving the quality of the products in order to keep assured of the survival of the company.

My advice was accepted; they returned to the mill and under Joe's leadership and with the full cooperation of management, set about in a most thorough and systematic manner to do just what I had suggested.

The local union did not immediately press requests for higher wages and other improvements. Within a few months, as a result of the sustained cooperative efforts of the workers and management, costs were reduced notably, and the quality of products improved. Even with its obsolete equipment the company survived and was able to grant the wage increases and improved conditions of employment already granted by their more prosperous competitors.

The employees were rightfully proud of their part in this effort to assure the survival of the company and so to preserve their jobs. Management was equally proud of the dramatic but practical result of teamwork. Thus was the foundation laid for building what has since come to be known as the Scanlon Plan.

Last October I participated in the ceremonies during which a memorial plaque in honor of Joe Scanlon was unveiled and dedicated at the Lapointe Machine Tool Company plant in Hudson, Massachusetts. Local Union No. 3536, United Steelworkers of America, consisting of all the employees of that company and the company management jointly arranged to have the plaque designed and produced. I want to repeat, in part, what I said at that time:

Thus the groundwork for a new and more creative concept of union-management relations was laid. As the news of this achievement spread and because it represented a departure from the traditional concept of a union's function and responsibilities, it was greeted with skepticism in some quarters and with enthusiasm in others.

It also led to increasing demands from both union members and harassed management officials for Joe Scanlon's help in putting their relations on a similar cooperative basis. As a result, it was finally decided to establish what came to be formally known as the Production Engineering Department of the United Steelworkers of America, with Joe Scanlon as Director. In this capacity Joe was able to not only extend the principles of union-management cooperation, which were gradually emerging out of trial and error in a growing number of enterprises, but also to greatly enhance the prestige and influence of the union throughout the basic steel and metal fabricating industries. Unions and management in other quite unrelated industries also sought his help and guidance.

Unfortunately the polluted atmosphere, which a great deal of the time then enveloped Pittsburgh, seriously affected his health. Seeking relief in a different environment, he accepted appointment to the staff of the Industrial Relations Section at the Massachusetts Institute of Technology. Here he was afforded wider opportunities to serve both management and unions and to expose some of the graduate students to the practical application of the principles of participation and union-management cooperation. Although his own academic background was limited, he won the respect of highly educated scholars and academicians. His unique talents were recognized by all associated with him at M.I.T.

It was at M.I.T. that Jack Ali and Ed Dowd and their pioneering associates in management and among the employees of Lapointe first sought and secured Joe Scanlon's advice and assistance. There is no need for me to recite the benefits that have come from this stimulating and fruitful association. In a very real sense, the people at Lapointe provided the laboratory in which the ideas and techniques evolved by Joe Scanlon have been tested, refined, and applied. As he so freely shared his knowledge and experience with you, so you, the Lapointe management and employees, have generously shared your accumulated experience with others. You have received visitors from abroad as well as from many parts of our own country, who were seeking ways to establish better relationships in their enterprises. Many enterprises, whose survival was threatened by unsatisfactory labor relations and resulting high costs, were literally saved from extinction by Joe Scanlon's successful efforts to put their union-management relations on a truly cooperative basis. His knowledge of manufacturing techniques and cost-accounting methods combined with extraordinary persuasive ability, enabled him to blaze new paths in the area of union-management relations.

For his constructive efforts, he earned the everlasting confidence and affection of the management people and the thousands of workers with whom he came in contact. A new and more responsible role for unions in the industrial relationship has been outlined by his pioneering work. Now that our unions have become more securely established, the significance of his work is likely to have greater recognition.

Joe Scanlon was an American worker with a deeply rooted faith in democracy and democratic processes. He believed that democracy, while not perfect, is perfectible and that democratic processes should be extended beyond purely politial governmental areas into industry and into all activities that will enable people to participate to the limit of their individual capabilities. In the workplaces, he believed that every worker, no matter how humble and seemingly unimportant his task, is capable of making a contribution not only to the success of the enterprise but to the happiness and well-being of his fellows. He believed that to the extent that workers are encouraged and enabled to make such contributions they will acquire the self-respect and self-confidence, the personal recognition and dignity which all normal people naturally seek.

Joe Scanlon was an unassuming, lovable, and unselfish human being, richly endowed by his Creator with the ability to serve rather than to command. His strength of mind was teamed with a greatness of heart. He was a generous and graceful giver and helper. He rejoiced when he saw others able to help themselves. He was a humble man. He sought neither recognition nor distinction. Both came to him nevertheless, as a result of his love and service to his fellow men.

He loved his country, he was proud of the heroic past, dissatisfied with the present, and confident of the future.

I have known many, many friends—I have clasped the hands of many that I loved, but in the long journey of my life, I have never grasped the hand of a better, truer, more unselfish friend than Joe Scanlon. It is quite unusual, I think, for the corporate management and union members to jointly honor a devoted trade unionist. Those of you who today constitute the management of the Lapointe Machine Tool Company and the membership of Local Union No. 3536 are living symbols of the wholesome type of cooperative effort that Joe Scanlon visualized and helped to make a fruitful reality.

It is eminently fitting, therefore, that you should join hands in providing the plaque to be unveiled today, which will honor and perpetuate the memory of an unselfish, humble worker who achieved distinction by helping others to help themselves.

2 ..

The Significance of Scanlon's Contribution

I have been thinking about three remarkable men whom I have had the privilege to know during my lifetime. One of them was a Jew who came out of the ghettos of Europe. He was born before the turn of the century, became a professor of psychology at the University of Berlin, left there along with Albert Einstein back in the early Thirties when the handwriting on the wall became clear. He lived and worked in this country until his death about ten years ago. He was a remarkable innovator—a man who has had as much influence as any man in his profession on the field of psychology during the last generation. His name was Kurt Lewin, and he was the father of what we now refer to as *group dynamics*—the study of what goes on in the face-to-face group and of the kinds of things that effect productivity and effectiveness and group morale.

The second man was an Ohio farm boy, also born in the last century, who at eighty today is a multimillionaire, a very famous man, also an innovator. He has had a profound influence on our society. His name is Charles Kettering, and he was research director of General Motors for many years. I know him because he was on the Board of Trustees of Antioch College where I was for a number of years, and I spent many hours sitting in my office discussing life with Ket.

The third man was an Irish lad of humble origin who was a prize fighter and a cost accountant; later he went to work in a steel mill, became a local-union president, then research director of the United Steelworkers of America, and finally a lecturer here at M.I.T. He was another innovator. I think time will show that he too has had a remarkable impact on our society. His name was Joseph Scanlon.

The differences between these three men are at first glance so great as to make you wonder why I even mention them in the same breath. But as I said, I have been struck with certain similarities among them which to me are impressive.

First of all, their point of view was always toward the future and never toward the past. Joe was fond of kidding people, sometimes quite seriously, about "facing the past and backing into the future." He had no use for the things that had been done, or for the milk that had been spilled; he wanted to look ahead and see what could come next. This was equally true of Kurt Lewin and is still true of Ket. Even at eighty, he is impatient with the way things are now being done, looking eagerly to what can happen next.

These three men, although they undertook things which were highly risky in terms of the chances of failure, never seemed to feel that risk was any more than an exciting challenge. The danger of failing never slowed them up, deterred them, or worried them. They were always emphasizing the chance of success. Kettering is fond of saying that he does not like the term "trial and error" because it carries the wrong implication. "You make trials, and you make mistakes, and you have errors, but you're aiming at success. What counts is the success that comes at the end of the road."

All three men had an experimental point of view. However, it was a rather unique one. It was not the experimental point of view of the physicist in the laboratory nearly so much as it was a practical concern with life itself. I have heard Ket say that with respect to the inventions in the automotive field that he has been concerned with, there were no formulas, no scientific laws that could give him the answers he was seeking. He had to turn to the engine. He said: "When you want to find out how to design a high-compression head, you can't find out with a slide rule how to cut the spaces in the head; you have to ask the engine—make a head, fit it on, and see how it runs."

Kurt Lewin was fond of what he called "action research." Though he fostered much research in the laboratory, he liked to get out into the field and deal experimentally with real-life situations. And Joe

Scanlon operated exclusively with this kind of experimental approach to the real life of industry.

None of these three men was ever intimidated by "what is known." There are many things in books that are not so. Those who are wise enough to realize this do not depend too heavily on the books for their answers. Again I think of many stories I have heard Ket tell about his experiences, for example, with the diesel engine. He was told by physical scientists at eminent institutions that the ideas he was working with were impossible—that he could not design an engine to do the things he was asking an engine to do. Ket tells with some amusement about talking to famous physicists about the principles that he finally used in the design of the diesel engine, about hearing them say they wouldn't work, at a time when Ket was able to reply: "There goes one down the track."

Kurt Lewin was the same way in his work with groups. If he had depended exclusively on what was in the books, he probably would have been deterred even before he started in the important work which he carried on. In the books he could find a lot about how a group was simply a collection of individuals, that all he needed to do was study them individually and then put them together, and that the sum of their individual efforts would give him his answers. Kurt knew from his observations of life that a group was more than a sum of individuals; his experiments helped to prove this and to show why. He contributed to human knowledge because he was able to put the books in perspective, read them, but not be intimidated by them.

In the same way, Joe, with his approach (for example, to the problems of incentives) was not a bit intimidated by the fact that we have thousands of volumes on incentives and on industrial-engineering practices related to them. He was prepared to go beyond these because his knowledge of life was such that he knew the books did not have all the answers.

I remember one experience with Kettering along this line which illustrates how he felt about this whole matter. I went to him for financial help for Antioch, and after some discussion he agreed to give us a library. The very fact that Ket would give a library was in itself an interesting thing. When I was talking with him later, when the library was being designed, I said: "Ket, what do you want inscribed over the door?" He looked at me for a moment, and then he grinned as he said: "You won't do it, but I'll tell you what I'd like over the door—Enter Here at Your Own Risk."

His research over the years included much that was going on at the Antioch campus under Ket's auspices. He had people studying about why plants are green—the subject of photosynthesis—which Ket believes in the long run is going to lead us to an understanding of sources of energy that will make atomic energy look like peanuts. This research is still in its early phases, but it is being actively pursued in the Kettering Laboratory at Antioch, among other places. Ket's way of handling his staff on this project reflected this same idea. Whenever they hit on a new notion of something to do experimentally, he would say: "Let's try it first, and then go see if other people have done it." The normal process is the reverse of this. His fear was that in going too soon to see what was in the books his staff might put on blinders and never see the possibilities. This was also a characteristic of Joe that I very much admired.

There are two other qualities about these three people that have stuck in my mind and they are far more important than any I have mentioned so far. One was an abiding faith in their fellow men. They did not see themselves as elite and the rest of the world as a mass of ignorant people. Each of these three great men was simply a human being in his dealings with other people. (I speak of Ket in the past tense, but at eighty he is still as alive and active as a man can be. The other two having passed on, it is difficult to use the right tense in referring to all three.)

I remember an experience Kettering had when a ship was being built and one of his first diesel engines was being installed in it. As he was wandering around the shipyard just a few weeks before the launching, he noticed one of the workmen standing at the stern of this vessel looking at it. Ket walked up to him, got into a conversation with him, hauled up a nail keg, and sat down for a while. He had noticed the man staring intently at the stern of the ship and finally asked: "What are you looking at?" The fellow said: "That propeller." Ket said: "What about it?" He said: "It's too big." Ket said: "How much too big?" "Oh," he said, "at least five inches; maybe five and a half."

I think most people would have dismissed such a comment at this point. This was an ordinary workman; he was not a member of management; he was not an architect—just an ordinary guy. But Ket did not drop the subject. He called up the architects and asked them to check the plans and find out the diameter of the propeller on this ship. They did and after a little while came back with an answer. Then he said: "Will you send somebody out to measure it?" And of course they did. Somewhat later he got a phone call, very shamefacedly, from the architectural firm. They said they did not know who had made the mistake, but the diameter of that propeller was five and a quarter inches too great! Under the conditions of design of this ship, this was a serious error. This kind of belief in the intelligence of his fellow men was as characteristic of Joe Scanlon and Kurt Lewin as it is of Kettering.

Finally, all of these things I have mentioned indicate to me in these three people, as in others like them, a way of life, a personal philosophy, and a view of what people are like and how one deals with them. This "philosophy" leads to an attitude toward risk and mistake making, to an optimism about what can be done, a refusal to think that anything is impossible, no matter how difficult it looks. It seems to me that even though the differences are sharp, the similarities among these three innovative men are worth some reflection.

Several people have raised a question with me when the Scanlon Plan has been under discussion. They have asked: "Why is it, if the Scanlon Plan is so good, that it isn't more widely adopted?" I should like to comment just a moment on this. If you as management are considering the development of a new product or process in industry, you expect without question to devote a lot of time, money, and energy to turning your initial idea into a working process or a finished product that can go on the market. The initial idea is very remote from the final product that appears on the market.

However, when we turn to look at the problems of managing people or to matters having to do with the organization of human effort, we find management attempting (quite unconsciously, I think) to shortcut this process completely and to assume that you can go from the original idea directly to the sale or use of the product without any intervening development process. For me, the growth of the Scanlon Plan since the middle Thirties represents a kind of development research that is still far from complete. This research has gone on in many companies rather than in one. There have been mistakes, there has been a lot of money, time, and energy put into it, and there will have to be a lot more before we realize the full potential of this complex and intricate set of ideas involved in Joe Scanlon's philosophy.

I have heard, over the days of the conference here, a number of questions implying that you wanted to have all the uncertainty taken out. Some of you seem to be saying: "If it's a good idea, tell me the gimmick; tell me how I can do it without any fear of failure; tell me how I can remove all the possible mistakes so that, when I go home and attempt to apply it, there'll be no risk involved." Now nobody said this in so many words, but this was the implication I got from some of the things that you said to each other. I should like to urge you to consider my analogy and realize that we are still at the pilot-plant stage. These things we are talking about—this way of life, if you like—which are represented by Scanlon and his ideas, are still being developed. There is still risk for the innovators. The implication of this is that you are being asked to go out on the end of a springboard to jump off in pitch darkness, not knowing whether there is water or rocks underneath you. I don't think this is the case either.

Over the years, the thing that has fascinated me most about Joe Scanlon and the pilot plants which some of you have been operating is the similarity between the insights that you are developing and some of the ideas that have been coming out of research in the social sciences focused on people. The way these insights have coincided with our increasing scientific knowledge in this field has been to me an exciting and fascinating thing to follow. I should like to mention before I close just a few that have struck me particularly because of the parallel between the Scanlon Plan and what is going on—entirely independent of Scanlon's operations—within the social-science field and within the field of management, broadly.

First consider with me the knowledge and the insights that we have acquired within the last fifteen or twenty years about delegation and decentralization within industrial organizations. We have learned that, if we push decision-making down in an organization as far as we possibly can, we tend to get better decisions, people tend to grow and to develop more rapidly, and they are motivated more effectively. Most companies today of any size at all are persuaded that the principles of decentralization and delegation—applied with wisdom—are fundamental to the successful operation of their organizations. We recognize that no small group of management or no single manager can have all the answers; even if he does have them, he will lose a great deal if he attempts to make all the decisions. He will never have an organization that grows and becomes healthy in its own right.

For me this idea, although unrelated to the Scanlon Plan, is remarkably similar in some of its implications. What Joe Scanlon was driving for was broad decentralization and genuine delegation, clear to the bottom of the organization. Some of you have given evidence of what happens when this idea is applied in that way.

There have been many developments in the social sciences in the last fifteen to twenty years having to do with motivation. We are coming around to very different notions about why people behave the way they do and about what motivates them. I am not going into this matter here, but I should like to mention that there has been much more evidence than we ever had before concerning the importance of the *social* motives of human beings. Man is still tremendously motivated to work with his fellows, to gain their recognition, their acceptance; the motivations existent in a social group are powerful in influencing behavior.

Those of you who knew Joe have heard him say many times that these social motivations, with their constructive and positive implications, have a great deal to offer management and workers alike. They are far more effective than what Joe called the "vicious" motivations stimulated by our attempt to use the carrot and stick with the typical individual incentive approach to motivation.

We have learned a great deal in recent years about the organization of work, and we have come to realize that the typical industrial-engineering approach—the "scientific-management" approach—of the last half century, which takes all the human elements out of work and turns man essentially into a glorified machine tool, is a waste of the most important resource of the organization. You see today in the concept of job enlargement and similar ideas (again entirely divorced from the Scanlon Plan) the same concern with using the knowledge, the skill, the ingenuity, and the ability of the individual with respect to his own job, and the same concern with building responsibility back into jobs that we have defined far too narrowly.

We have had at M.I.T. for a number of years an activity that some people might regard as industrial engineering. The faculty members who head it refer to it as "the management of improvement." They have made a sharp break with traditional industrial-engineering approaches. They are concerned with participative methods that can be used to improve performance on the job. Here is something right here at M.I.T. which has been completely independent of the Scanlon Plan but which has gone parallel with it to a remarkable degree.

Finally, there is one other independent development which parallels Joe's work. It is the notion that, by and large, people are capable of being mature adults in their relationships with each other—that they are capable of *self*-direction, of *self*-discipline, of *self*-control. Our whole managerial philosophy for the past several centuries has been built on the notion that people are like children, incapable of directing their own activities within the organization, incapable of controlling and disciplining themselves. If we take this point of view, the task of management must be that of directing them, manipulating them, and controlling them in doing the job that has to be done.

I think we are beginning to get evidence from a variety of sources that this is not true, and I suspect that our conception of management as a manipulative, directive process is one day going to be supplanted by a very different notion that people are, after all, adults and capable of self-direction. When we begin to treat them that way, we shall have some different consequences in organizational behavior.

Much of the behavior we see in typical industrial organizations today is not a consequence of human nature; it is a consequence of the way we organize, of the way we manage people. Resistance to output, antagonism to management, and all kinds of subtle ways of defeating the purposes of the organization are not inherent expressions of human nature; they are results—consequences of the fact that we have built organizations and methods of control that bring about exactly these behaviors.

We have evidence in the companies that are experimenting with the Scanlon Plan concerning the different behavior you begin to get when you set up a different kind of organization with a different management philosophy, based on the idea that people are, after all, capable of behaving like adults. We have heard illustration after illustration which on the surface sound pretty odd. Says one man: "We don't have fights any more about moving a man from this operation to that one. He doesn't quarrel about the limits of his job; we don't have to go back to the contract to see whether he can be moved around." We have heard examples of people helping each other on their jobs. When one fellow runs out of work he goes over and helps another man on with his job. We have been told that the issue of management prerogatives has ceased to be an issue.

To my way of thinking what really is being said is that when we set up a different way of life in the industrial organization, we can expect people to behave differently. And this is exactly what some of you have discovered. It looks strange to those on the outside whose experience has been different. Perhaps it explains why some of us are worried about the legal limits we would have to put on the Scanlon agreement to make sure that this or that or the other thing does not happen. We are habituated to seeing people respond in certain ways to the typical managerial philosophy that we have been using for so long.

I should mention before I close one important caution to any of you who perhaps are thinking of shifting in the direction of this different way of life, this way of treating people as if they were capable adults. It is simply this: we can't learn to run until we learn to walk. It takes time and lots of mistakes before we can grow from the pattern that we may be accustomed to, of treating people like children and having them respond like children, to the pattern of having them react like adults.

It's easy enough, of course, to use this as an excuse to continue past practices. But even if you adopt a way of life that is built on a genuine belief that people can grow, can learn together, and can solve their mutual problems together, you must still expect the process to take some time. And the spotty picture that we have seen among the companies represented here—different degrees of success and failure, different experiences, different kinds of mistakes that have been lived through—simply reflects this natural but difficult process of growth and development which goes on when one attempts to practice a new managerial philosophy.

I should like to close by reminding you once more of my initial comment about the three men: Kurt Lewin, Charles Kettering, Joe Scanlon. In my honest opinion these were three great men. They had many qualities of greatness among them, but the most important one, the one that will make them stand out through the years, was their abiding conviction that they and their fellow men together could achieve the impossible.

PART TWO . . . .

The Plan

RUSSELL W. DAVENPORT

3 . . . .

Enterprise for Everyman

There is nothing about the Lapointe Machine Tool Company that would lead the visitor to suspect that it houses the makings of a far-reaching management-labor revolution. It is a small, neat factory in Hudson, Massachusetts, where the executives walk up three flights to get to their varnished offices and most of the 350 employees eat lunch at home because they live nearby. Founded in 1903 by a French-Canadian named La Pointe, it was later purchased by John J. Prindiville, whose son, big, six-foot-six John Jr., is now President and owner of the equity stock. It is a modest enterprise with a reputation for high quality; there is even a trace of modesty in its boast that it is "the world's oldest and largest manufacturer of broaches and broaching machines." Yet the social achievement at Lapointe is something to make one pause and consider, for the discoveries that its management and union have made concerning the enterprise system could have repercussions around the civilized world.

Labor relations at Lapointe were never "bad"—yet they were not "good" either. They were just about like labor relations anywhere

Reprinted by special permission from the January 1950 issue of *Fortune*. Copyrighted 1950 by Time, Inc.

else, which is to say that there was mistrust on both sides leading on occasion to ill will. There was constant trouble, for example, over the piecework incentive system. Some rates were so easy that the men earned big bonuses and had to hold back production lest the rates be cut. Others were so hard that only the most skillful could earn any bonus at all. The indirect workers had no incentive rate and resented those of the others. Grievances abounded—the union was processing fifteen or twenty a month. There were numerous production delays, spoilage was too high, and deliveries were bad. In short, the picture was a typical one as industrial relations go—worse than some, not so bad as others.

In 1945 the plant was organized by the United Steelworkers, and about a year thereafter the Steelworkers called a national strike for a postwar wage increase. The Lapointe contract still had six months to run, and many of the men didn't want to go out anyway. However, the decision was to strike. Management thereupon sought an injunction, on the ground that the contract had been violated, and won a favorable decision from Judge Charles C. Cabot of the Massachusetts Superior Court. The union was enjoined from picketing the plant or otherwise interfering with operations. Early in April the strike at Lapointe ended. But there was bitterness in the air, and the situation was not improved by the realization that the machine-tool industry, after its war boom, had fallen on lean times. The unsettling possibility of a layoff hovered constantly over the shop.

It so happened about this time that Jack Ali, then president of the union, picked up a copy of *Life* (December 23, 1946) and his eye fell on an article by John Chamberlain with the intriguing title of "Every Man a Capitalist." Mr. Ali read it. It told about a small maker of steel tanks called the Adamson Company, where union and management had come together to install an amazing productivity plan, with the result that the company's profitability had increased two and a half times and the men had taken home bonuses ranging up to 54 per cent of a high basic wage. The author of the plan was one Joseph Scanlon, of whom Mr. Ali had never heard. However, he took the article to the union executive committee and together they became tremendously excited. After two evenings' discussion, the committee got in touch with Executive Vice President Edward M. Dowd, second-in-command to Mr. Prindiville—a big man, up from the ranks, whose intimate knowledge of the broaching business is matched only by his sure-footed understanding of the men in his shop: Mr. Dowd turned a willing ear to what the committee had to say and on reading the article was deeply stirred.

There then followed some very active weeks. Messrs. Dowd and Ali journeyed out to East Palestine, Ohio, where they went over the Adamson plan in detail. They discovered that Mr. Scanlon was now teaching at M.I.T., scarcely forty miles from Hudson, and they presently made their appearance in his office. Mr. Scanlon, in turn, sent them to Roy Stevens, the regional field representative of the United Steelworkers. When they had obtained this gentleman's blessing they returned to the Scanlon office and began to dig down to bedrock. In the meantime Mr. Dowd had had frequent conferences with Mr. Prindiville, who was at once interested, and after some deliberation gave them the green light. Negotiations with the union were begun. And by December 1, 1947, the Scanlon Plan was installed at Lapointe.

The Scanlon Development

Now the Adamson experiment that started this chain of events was no mere accident in labor-management relations. It had its roots in the painful Thirties, when a group of labor leaders in the steel country evolved certain principles that have within them the power to revolutionize labor's relationship to enterprise, and vice versa. One of these leaders was Joseph Scanlon, whose versatile career included cost accounting, a spell as a professional boxer, a return to cost accounting (his basic profession), and then a shift over to the production side as an open-hearth worker. In 1936, during the formation of the S.W.O.C., Mr. Scanlon was on the open hearth of a marginal steel company, where he took a leading part in the organizing drive and was elected president of the new local.

Like many other steel manufacturers, this company was close to the rocks in 1938. Costs were high, the ink was red, liquidation seemed inevitable. Mr. Scanlon and his fellow union officers felt that something had to be done. They persuaded the president of the company to join with them in a visit to Pittsburgh to see Clinton Golden, then vice president of the Steelworkers and Phil Murray's good right arm. Mr. Golden had long been preaching a gospel of cooperation between management and labor for the good of both; nevertheless, he received this contingent with some degree of astonishment. Said he afterward, "The union headquarters in those days was about as popular a place for industrial executives to visit as a pesthouse. I was immediately impressed by the fact there was something extraordinary happening here."

Mr. Golden advised them to go back and try to work out a plan by which union and management could join together to save the enterprise. And the upshot was a pioneer union-management productivity plan, which provided that the workers would get a bonus for tangible savings in labor costs. Despite the fact that the primary aim of this plan was merely *survival,* it worked almost like magic and became the seed of all of Mr. Scanlon's future work. Costs were cut so much that the company actually began to make a profit, and the workers got a bonus to boot. One suggestion by the union production committee, for example, cost less than $8,000 in new equipment but saved about $150,000 in one year.

Scores of other companies doing business with the union found themselves in this same tough position in the late Thirties. Primarily to save the jobs of union members, Messrs. Murray and Golden brought Mr. Scanlon into the national headquarters to work on these cases. Sometimes at the request of the company, often at that of the union, productivity plans based upon union-management cooperation were installed in forty to fifty companies. The largest of these early-period plans was at a basic steel company employing about 4,000 people; the smallest was at a water-heater company with 150 employees. According to Mr. Scanlon, "The successes were just as marked in the larger companies as in the small ones."

Out of this work came a book—*The Dynamics of Industrial Democracy,* by Clinton S. Golden and Harold J. Ruttenberg—and a proposition. The proposition was that collective bargaining, as thus far developed, was a primitive affair and that the future task of labor and management would be to evolve a more mature relationship. In this new relationship collective bargaining would include, not merely wages, hours, working conditions, etc., but intelligent cooperation between the bargaining parties. Such cooperation could not be expected if the workers were shoved to one side, kept ignorant of the business, and treated as pawns in a game going on over their heads. A new principle must be introduced, which has since come to be called the principle of *participation.*

Last October [1949], in the first article of the present series, "The Greatest Opportunity on Earth," this principle was referred to as the most important area in which to implement the economic rights that the article set forth. But, unfortunately, when he uses the word participation, the average executive usually has something rather superficial in mind. He seeks to develop in the worker a *feeling* of participation, a *sense* of belonging. But is this quite honest? To make the worker feel that he is participating without giving him a real participation is, after all, to fool him; and deception is a flimsy, not to say an inflammable, foundation for industrial relations. Real participation consists in finding a means by which to reward labor for any increase in productivity and *then in building around this formula a working relationship between management and labor that enables them to become a team.* Once a team has been established, it is found that labor's prime interest, just like that of management, becomes *productivity.*

Such, at any rate, was the fruitful vein that Messrs. Dowd and Ali had come upon at the Adamson Company, the most spectacular of the Scanlon developments. The performance of Adamson, indeed, had attracted the attention of Douglas McGregor, then head of the industrial-relations section at M.I.T., now president of Antioch College; and Mr. McGregor had persuaded Mr. Scanlon to come to M.I.T. There, with the help of economists, engineers, statisticians, and other experts on the M.I.T. faculty, Mr. Scanlon's work has entered a new phase, in which he can draw upon his vast experience in the labor-management field to give advice in the installation of real participation plans to those companies that seek him out.

The Formula

The first task in the application of the Scanlon plan is to find a "normal" labor cost for the plant under consideration and then to devise a means for giving labor the benefit of anything it can save under that "norm." In every case, therefore, some kind of link must be found between the worker and over-all shop productivity. Because every company is different, the nature of this link differs in almost every case; and because labor usually objects to having its costs accurately measured, some of the accounting handles that Mr. Scanlon has used are rather weird. At a manufacturer of silverware it is ounces of silver processed; at a wholesale warehouse it is tons warehoused; at a steel foundry and machine shop in the Deep South it is pounds of castings produced. At the Market Forge Company, a versatile steel-fabricating shop in Everett, Massachusetts, it is a calculated percentage of operating profits per month.

This last method, linking laborsaving to the profit and loss statement, is of course the basis of many profit-sharing plans. But Mr. Scanlon feels, and Market Forge itself agrees, that it is the least desirable of any of the links, because the connection between the worker's productive efficiency and the final profit is too remote for many to grasp. It was adopted at Market Forge because the types of jobs coming into that shop are so variable that a labor-cost figure was impossible to determine. Notwithstanding this seeming weakness, a high level of participation has been developed at Market Forge, where more than 300 recorded suggestions for improved productivity have been put into effect in the past two years.

At Lapointe, where measurement was relatively easy, Mr. Scanlon decided on the most direct and understandable accounting handle—the ratio of labor cost to total production value, the latter figure being equal to monthly sales plus or minus the change in inventory. Since this labor ratio is a highly competitive figure, Lapointe will not make it public. However, the principle can be illustrated, and all the Lapointe moves intelligently followed, by taking the average for the whole machine-tool industry. According to the Department of Commerce the ratio of wages and salaries to the value of shipments for the entire industry for 1947 was 40.7 per cent—which, to speak in round figures, we may call 41 per cent. In actuality, the company felt that the "norm" derived from its war records was too high, and the union consequently agreed to a reduction of three points. If this were applied to the industry-wide average, the norm would be 38 per cent, and the plan would work as follows. If total shipments for a given month were 70,000, and inventory change was plus $30,000, total production value would be $100,000 for that month. The "normal" payroll would then be calculated at 38 per cent, or $38,000. If the actual payroll were only $35,000, the difference of $3000 would go to the workers as their bonus.

Several important points are to be noted regarding this approach. First, labor gets *all* of the laborsaving; management's profit from the plan is derived from increased sales with no corresponding increase in total "burden" (i.e., overhead and labor costs). Second—and absolutely basic to the Scanlon system—the bonus is given to all the workers and not just to those individuals who made productivity suggestions. At Market Forge it goes to every person in the business, including Leo M. Beckwith, the owner—and Mr. Scanlon prefers this setup. At Lapointe, however, it goes to all except the fourteen top executives, who have a bonus system of their own, based on sales. Lapointe distributes the Scanlon bonus to every individual every month, as a calculated percentage of his basic rate—that is, his hourly, weekly, or monthly pay.

Mr. Scanlon believes that the broadest and most meaningful participation requires a union—in the two or three instances where he has proceeded without one there have been delays and difficulties that a union would have helped to untangle. A firm distinction is made, however, between ordinary union affairs and the productivity affairs; grievances, for example, are handled through the grievance committee and are never discussed in the union-management productivity committees. Preferably, the original suggestion to try the plan should come from the union (as at Lapointe); but if it comes from management, the consent of the union must certainly be obtained, together with the approval of the regional representative. In many instances the plan rests on a simple "memorandum of agreement"; at Lapointe it is actually part of the collective-bargaining contract.

Thus the basic theory is that labor should profit from laborsavings, while the company profits from a better use of its assets (for example, lower unit costs). And in order to maintain this dynamic balance at the original point agreed upon, it is provided that changes can be made in the formula to compensate for changed conditions on either side. Thus, some weeks after the plan actually went into effect, management decided to cut prices by 10 per cent on about half the products. Since this would result in a decrease in production value from a nonlabor source, about three points had to be *added* to labor's norm. This would bring our average norm for the industry back to 41 per cent. If management were to raise prices, the opposite adjustment would have to be made.

If a further general rise in wages were to occur, the union at Lapointe would insist that the workers get it in their wage rates; one of Mr. Scanlon's cardinal principles is that a productivity bonus must not be used as a substitute for a wage increase. But again, in order to maintain the dynamic balance, such a change in the wage level, since it would be an additional labor cost, would require a revision of the norm, here, too, upward. The change can be avoided in only two ways: (1) management may pass the increase along in the form of increased prices, in which event the labor ratio to sales will remain the same; or (2) consideration for the company's competitive position may induce labor to absorb part or all of the increase by agreeing to let the ratio stand as it was. Thus at Lapointe the union and the company undertook to eliminate basic wage inequities, and this resulted in a sizable increase in payroll. Since, however, this cost could not be passed along in prices and still keep the business at a good volume, labor consented to the maintenance of the original norm (41 per cent by our hypothetical figure), instead of insisting on a larger share of the sales dollar. In effect, therefore, the increase in payroll cost came out of increased productivity; and since prices did not go up, the customers of Lapointe were the chief beneficiaries of the difference. This benefit to the customers comes back, in turn, to the company in the form of more secure jobs and profits.

On the other hand, there is built into the agreement a provision that where management makes an investment that will raise labor productivity, without any increased work on the part of the labor force, such investment may entail a recalculation of labor's norm, this time downward. Lapointe has, in fact, invested in about forty major pieces of equipment in the past year. It is impossible to tell how much of this is actually new investment and how much is in reality replacement, though the total would run to six figures. Nevertheless, management feels that this investment is to some extent a fair exchange for labor's extra rise in productivity and has not therefore exercised this provision of the agreement.

All this is collective bargaining of a high order, brought about by the participation principle. The entire factory competes, from the ground up. Because management sees its best hope in the cooperation of the workers, it decides to forgo claims that it would otherwise exact. And because the workers know the company's competitive problem in detail, their bargaining for labor's share is oriented to that problem.

One more provision was needed at Lapointe to put the plan in balance. Three times in the first two years the productivity curve has dipped below the norm—that is, labor costs were *greater* than our hypothetical average of 41 per cent. The company had paid out bonuses for the gains; who was to reimburse it for the losses? Owing to the extraordinary understanding that is developed by participation, the men were quick to see the injustice that was being worked on the company, and even though the contract contained no such provision, the union voluntarily agreed to an adjustment. The final arrangement was that the company should hold back half of the first 15 per cent of each month's bonus to take care of possible months when the payroll was greater than labor's norm. This amount is kept in a reserve fund, and whatever is left is distributed at the end of each year.

The reserve has had a salutary effect. It gives management a reasonable protection against temporary but unforeseeable slumps. On the other hand, it gives the workers a better perspective on the business. The desire to protect the reserve gives them the same dread of red ink that management has.

Implementation of the Formula

The increased productivity of the shop under the Scanlon system is not achieved by a "speed-up" in the ordinary sense of the word. Possibly the men work harder, and certainly they work more steadily, but the rise in efficiency is brought about chiefly by suggestions as to how time and effort can be saved. These suggestions are handled by shop committees, called "production committees," whose members are always on the job and easily accessible. They are empowered to put any suggestion into effect that does not involve some other department or a substantial outlay of money. Over the production committees there sits the screening committee, composed of representatives of management and labor from the various departments, which rules on suggestions of wider scope. Each suggestion is carefully tagged with the name of the person making it; if it is accepted, some member of the committee is specifically assigned the job of following it up; if rejected, someone is instructed to make a thorough explanation to the worker. At Lapointe the screening committee has received 513 suggestions in twenty-four months. Of these, 380 have been accepted, 28 started, 32 are pending, and 65 have been rejected.

Employers who have installed a casual "suggestion box" system in their plants can have little idea of the kind of thing that goes on in a Scanlon Plan committee. For that matter, the average employer has little conception of the wealth of imagination and ingenuity lying untapped in the heads of the workmen. Under conventional management such ideas are blocked by a number of factors. A worker who has an idea may be given no incentive to suggest it. But even if there is an incentive, he may decide to withhold it, rather than incur the enmity or jealousy of his fellow workers, and especially of his foreman, who may construe the idea as a criticism of his own management. The individual is frustrated; and, moreover, since he can see how a saving could be made, and since management obviously does not see it, his respect for management declines. Add to this the fact that his communications with management are virtually nil. He has no idea of company problems, and hence no idea of why some moves are made that seem to him (and may in fact be) very stupid.

All this is fertile ground for the kind of animosity that has grown up in some labor circles against what the managers advocate as "free enterprise." Indeed, a number of workers at Lapointe, who feel that they can now talk with freedom, admit that in the old pre-Plan days they never associated themselves or their jobs with the profits of the company and maybe even got a little kick when they heard that the top floor was using red ink.

If one steps from that kind of shop, which often exists even under what is ordinarily called "good" management, and takes one's seat as an observer at a Scanlon Plan screening committee, one passes, with Alice, through the looking glass and into an entirely different world. Like a crack out of a gun the meeting opens with an announcement of the figures for the past month. There follows a roundup by management of the current situation of the company. Then the suggestions are read out, one by one, and debated. A lot of criticism is generated and is of necessity accepted, since it is all directed to the same end—a better profit. Sometimes the workers throw the book at management, sometimes management points out where the shop has fallen down. Engineers argue against machine-tool operators, foremen attack the engineers for unrealistic blueprints, someone demands better maintenance, management points out that more maintenance means bigger labor costs. In the process of this debate, almost every aspect of the business comes up for discussion—sales problems, competitors, orders, bids, spoilage, the business outlook, quality of materials, customers' foibles, management difficulties, etc. The result is a dynamic, working unity, which grows out of the bargaining table and yet wholly transcends it. The sudden realization dawns that here at Lapointe *collective bargaining has come of age.*

The meetings are not recorded verbatim. But minutes are distributed to everyone in the plant, and the important points in the debate are carried by the committeemen back into the shop, where they become the subject of further discussion—at the lunch hour, in the evening, or even at the union meeting. The result is that everyone at Lapointe knows the business and takes pride in his particular contribution.

Company Benefits

The extraordinary results of this formula, implemented by the intimate labor-management committees, could make a long and fascinating tale. For our present purposes it will be necessary to concentrate on the most important.

First of all, the Plan has resulted in a good return to the owners. Since Lapointe does not publish its profit figures it is impossible to be precise about this.* The profits at Lapointe have not been so spectacular as those at Adamson—indeed it is probable that during the first year of the Plan the company made hardly any profit at all. This goes back to the nature of the machine-tool industry, which has been in something of a slump ever since the war. It is commonly accepted in the industry that Lapointe has been gaining an increasingly large percentage of the business ever since the Plan was inaugurated. During 1948 great strides were made at Lapointe in its ability to compete,

* The Kiplinger magazine recently published figures on Lapointe, but many were inaccurate and were denied by the company.

which may not have shown up immediately in the profit and loss statement. In 1949 the results have been much more tangible; in contrast to much of the industry the company is now operating at a good profit.

All of this improvement cannot be attributed to the productivity plan. Lapointe has a sharp-eyed management that has been quick to follow up new leads in the hitherto obscure broaching business. It has been rewarded by the fact that modern engineering is finding new uses for broaching—for instance, machine-gun barrels, which were formerly rifled at the rate of one an hour, can now be broached at the rate of sixty an hour. Moreover, an entirely new business is opening up through the fact that certain parts of jet engines cannot be efficiently manufactured except by broaching. These are long-range gains attributable to factors other than labor.

However, management and labor are now cooperating so effectively at Lapointe that it is impossible to tell where the contributions of one ends and that of the other begins. Certain intangible benefits have accrued from this teamwork that affect the company's whole operation. For example, there has been a vast improvement in deliveries. Formerly delivery on ordinary broaches had been from three to five weeks and was often late. Now delivery can be made in from one to three weeks and is usually on time. This has become a great selling point for the company.

A second advantage is the reduction in complaints from spoilage and imperfect workmanship. Lapointe's policy is to take back any unsatisfactory product and fix it without extra cost. Under the Scanlon Plan this means *a loss to the workers as well as to the company*, and as a result great care is taken all along the line. The workers, indeed, get very excited about the big jobs. In one instance, when a new machine for a big automobile manufacturer was being tried out in the Lapointe plant, several of the union committee left their own jobs and gathered around to see whether the automotive manufacturer's engineers were duly impressed. While losses from customer complaints probably never amounted to as much as 1 per cent of the business, the intangible result of satisfied customers willing to reorder is a real one, for which management can thank its own foresight in installing a plan that gives the workers an interest in their product.

Moreover, the problem of instructing younger workers has been greatly advanced. Formerly, under the piecework incentive system, a highly skilled workman was reluctant to show a younger man the tricks of his trade. But today the older workers are eager to teach their skills, in order to raise shop productivity. The most dramatic example at Lapointe was that of Robert Juliani, the best and most experienced form grinder, who made $3.57 an hour under the old piecework system. Formerly Mr. Juliani was given no incentive to share his knowledge and skill, but after the plan he reorganized his work, took on two helpers, and taught them many of his ways of doing things. It is estimated that his increased efficiency is in the neighborhood of 300 per cent.

The plan, indeed, has completely solved the problem of "controlled production"—that is, the policy, common to almost all labor, of holding back so that management will never know how fast a man really can work. The very first day it was installed a toolmaker, who had been producing twenty units in eight hours, produced sixty-two units. A surface grinder, whose average weekly earnings had been $76 on piecework, turned out $184 worth of work in four days. And so forth, through innumerable examples.

Labor Benefits

On labor's side the benefits have been equally great. The average pay at Lapointe is in line with basic steel for the region, and for two years the workers have taken home an average bonus of 18 per cent over and above this. The bonus has, naturally, varied widely, ranging from zero to 39 per cent in June, 1949. Even better results are expected in 1950.

But the workers, like management, have derived many intangible benefits that cannot be measured in dollars and cents. They seem to enjoy working together and sharing the good and bad times. As one of them said, "Formerly everyone was on his own. Now we all work for each other." Innumerable versions of this observation can be picked up around the plant. One can spend little time here without reflecting that one of the weaknesses of conventional management is its almost exclusive emphasis on the money incentive. For the money incentive cannot satisfy the many demands of human nature—and this goes for management as well as for labor. Other incentives are needed if a man is to lead a healthy and happy life. Among these, two are of the utmost importance. One has to do with one's self—a feeling of accomplishment, a recognition of one's own abilities. This is provided for in the Scanlon Plan through the suggestion system, because a man who makes a good suggestion gets a profound satisfaction out of it; he carries the story home to his wife; he is admired and thanked by his associates. But the Scanlon Plan goes further, in that the reward for such suggestions does not go to the individual alone but to the entire shop. On the one hand, this eliminates jealousy; on the other, it opens up for the ordinary worker a kind of social or community incentive to which he eagerly responds. Cynics to the contrary, men do get a kick out of helping their fellow men; and this is demonstrated at Lapointe, where an atmosphere prevails in the shop that cannot possibly be duplicated under the selfish piecework system.

Yet another intangible advantage that the workers have derived is a strengthening of the union. If any employer becomes interested in this plan as a means of undermining the union, he had better skip it. Mature collective bargaining that has reached the evolutionary stage here described has precisely the opposite result. When the Plan was installed, union membership at Lapointe was about 70 per cent of the working force, exclusive of the office workers, who were not organized. Today all but three or four employees are union members, and the office workers have joined in a body. Interest in the union is keen. The advantage of this from the employer's point of view is that union meetings, instead of being dominated by a few malcontents, are heavily attended; and often enough most of the discussion is devoted to company affairs and how productivity can be increased. The union president, energetic and imaginative Fred Lesieur, who has succeeded Mr. Ali, is enthusiastic about the Plan. The result of all this is that grievances have almost disappeared—only three have been processed in twenty-four months, and none of them has had to go to arbitration.

One of the greatest advantages of this kind of collective bargaining, from the worker's point of view, is the knowledge that it gives him of the business. When a slump is coming, he knows it. He is even given a chance to combat it, in the sense that if he can devise a cheaper way of turning out his product, perhaps the company will be able to take business away from somebody else. In a number of instances the Lapointe workers have actually done this, the most spectacular example being that of an order from a big automotive concern in December, 1948. The workers had been pressing management to accept orders even at the break-even point so as to tide over a bad period. Mr. Prindiville, who sometimes sits in on the screening-committee meetings, had given in to the pressure some months previously to the extent of taking an order from this firm for 100 broaches at $83 per broach. But Lapointe had lost 10 per cent on the deal, and Mr. Prindiville now put his foot down. If this business was to be taken again the price would have to be raised. In view of new competition, it meant that Lapointe almost certainly would not get the business—and at a time when work was scarce.

The gloomy gathering that listened to Mr. Prindiville's pronouncement was then electrified by a question from Jimmie McQuade, skilled grinder and one of the most outspoken members of the screening committee. Who says we can't make those broaches at that price for a profit? Mr. McQuade wanted to know. If you'd give the men in the shop a chance to go over the blueprints before production starts and to help plan the job, there are lots of ways of cutting costs without cutting quality. The idea grew, and the next day the suggestion ran around the shop like wildfire. The order was taken at the old price, this time with a *profit* of 10 per cent—a total gain in efficiency of 20 per cent.

The truth is that the Scanlon Plan has generated a competitive spirit throughout the factory: one hears as much about competition from the workers as from management itself. If there is a question of struggling for existence the whole company struggles collectively, and all the brains available are focused on the fight. The worker is no longer a pawn in a game he does not understand. He is a player. He enjoys it. And his contribution is worth money to all concerned.

The Team at Work

The effectiveness of such teamwork becomes especially apparent in the crises. Lapointe has been through three critical periods since the Plan was installed, and it has lifted itself out of them principally because the Plan creates an overwhelming incentive to cooperate.

The first crisis occurred in the fourth month. Mr. Scanlon had warned management that output would greatly increase and that they had better begin hustling up some new orders. But management had a normal backlog, and inasmuch as it was having trouble with deliveries it did not dare put on any extra sales pressure. The very first month, however, productivity shot up to 133 per cent (100 equals the predetermined "norm" already defined); the second month registered 128 per cent and the third 121 per cent. The result was that the company's backlog melted away. Management, of course, sprang to action as soon as the danger was realized. Telegrams and telephone calls poured out of Hudson. The salesmen were lashed to activity. Though himself a production man, Vice President Dowd—and even several engineers—took to the road. But broaches and broaching machines are technical tools that sometimes require weeks of designing before production can begin. Consequently the new orders did not give much immediate help, and the next three months were bad; the company ran a loss and the workers got no bonus.

Yet, as it turned out, the strength of the Plan was best demonstrated when things went bad. The workers had had three months of participation; they looked forward to bonuses in the future; and they liked the Plan because it gave them a *chance*—a chance to fight, a chance to pit their skills against other enterprises. Consequently, despite the setback, sentiment among them was overwhelming to continue the Plan, and suggestions kept pouring in for improvements. By June, 1948, a small bonus (4.7 per cent) was earned.

But then there was new trouble. The usual practice of the plant was to shut down for vacations for two weeks in July. Big new orders had come in, but these had to pass through the engineering department for designing, and when the engineers were on vacation no designing would be done. Would anybody dare to ask the engineers to give up their vacations?—especially in view of the fact that, as is usual in machine shops, there was continuous bickering between the engineers and the machine operators, who were inclined to criticize the drawings as unrealistic. A delegation from the union approached Vice President Dowd, who said that he would put it up to the men themselves. When he went to the men, however, he found that agreement had already been reached at the workers' level— the engineers had sacrificed their vacations. They worked hard during July in an otherwise empty plant, and by August drawings were pouring out of the drafting room. Productivity soared again, yielding a bonus of 25 per cent for September and 19 per cent for October. A better example of community incentive could hardly be found.

Still another difficulty then arose. The problem was to devise a machine capable of broaching certain parts of a jet airplane engine. Everybody had said the parts in question could not be broached, but the Lapointe engineers insisted they could be, providing a new machine was developed. The problem centered around a very hard steel, close to the limit for cutting tools, and the company's efforts to solve it resulted in many a setback. Labor watches every job at Lapointe, and the men became impatient when they saw so much work being done on which there would be no shipping dollars. But management went back to the screening committee again and again and said in effect, "Bear with us. This is experimental stuff. If we can get it right, we're in." So the screening committee went along. Then at last the bugs were out, production began, and everybody went to town. The monthly productivity curve shot up, from a dismal low of 71 per cent in December, 1948 (in the middle of the experimental work), to 119, 138, 140, 145, 150, and finally, in the twentieth month of the plan, to 161 per cent.

These three incidents provide three dramatic examples of teamwork. In the first, the workers held on despite an unexpected discouragement. In the second, the engineers came to the rescue of all concerned. In the third, management exercised its proper function with great intelligence, by insisting that temporary losses be sustained in order to grasp a future profit. If this experimental work had failed, a certain field of sales would have been closed to Lapointe. As it is, the firm got in on the ground floor of a new and growing business, and all concerned will profit from that achievement.

Will It Work for You?

Many objections will be raised to the Scanlon Plan by those who have never seen it in operation. But perhaps the least fruitful objection of all is the one most commonly encountered: "This plan may work at Lapointe—or wherever—but that is because of special, perhaps accidental, circumstances. *My* plant is different."

Of course, everybody's plant *is* different. Every union is different also. For this very reason Mr. Scanlon refuses to crystallize his work into a formula. He relies on certain principles fundamental to human nature; and he adapts these in almost infinite ways to the particular problems of each particular company. He has now met with success, in varying degrees, in more than fifty enterprises in several different industries, of many different sizes, under many different circumstances; where the original labor relations were good and where they were bad; where profits were good and where they were nonexistent; where labor productivity was easy to measure and where it was virtually impossible; among skilled workers and unskilled workers. There are, of course, shops where this plan would not work. But the burden of the evidence is accumulating that those in which it will not work are the *exceptions*.

Yet there are two prerequisites to the Scanlon Plan, and where they do not exist time would be wasted in trying to install it. One is that the union leadership must be intelligent. This does not mean that the union should be acquiescent: on the contrary, it may be quite aggressive. But real intelligence is needed to bargain at a participation level, which involves an understanding of such things as competition, competitive pricing, profitability, and many other factors that never enter into collective bargaining at the lower level. This prerequisite to Scanlon Plan success is provided at Lapointe by Fred Lesieur, the new union president, who, as a good union man, considers it his *responsibility* to have an intelligent grasp of the productivity side of the business. The other union officers share this responsibility.

Second, and even more important, there must be someone in top management who is vitally interested and *who is able to stand the gaff*. A management that wants to stand off and look down its nose at the workers cannot operate a Scanlon Plan. Nor is it possible to turn this vital area of the business over to a vice president in charge of industrial relations. Someone who actually runs the company or the plant—the president or his executive representative—must be a regular member of the screening committee (he need not be chairman); and this person must be willing to enter into any kind of debate and to accept in a fair and impartial manner any criticism hurled at his own management. He need not worry about his dignity. The men will invest him with the dignity he deserves—no more, but no less.

It is precisely in this respect that Lapointe has been so fortunate. Lapointe has in John Prindiville a man of open mind, who believes that the incentives of enterprise should reach down, through management, to the shop floor. And it has in Ed Dowd a man who became the Plan's prime mover, utterly dedicated to its goals. Mr. Dowd is not afraid of criticism—and is not afraid to give it. The men know he is sincere in his efforts to make the Plan work, and they consequently trust him. Besides, he sets quite a pace. When the argument gets hot, he takes off his coat, and everyone interprets this as permission to do likewise. Comfortably in his shirt sleeves, Ed Dowd pitches into the suggestions, throws upon each of them the light of his enormous knowledge of the business, tosses them back to the committee, and finally designates some individual to "follow it through." When there is a tough one involving important company policy, Ed Dowd takes it himself.

If such men can be found—an intelligent union leader and a forthright management leader—the Scanlon principles can be applied virtually anywhere. And the way is then opened up to a new and creative area of industrial relations—the area of mutual interests. In the process of entering upon this area, and of consolidating it, *everyone* in the shop, high or low, joins the enterprise system.

FREDERICK G. LESIEUR

4 . . . .

What the Plan Isn't and What It Is

The best way of describing the Scanlon Plan is the method used by Joe Scanlon on many occasions over the years before his death. This means spending just as much time telling you what the Plan isn't as what it is. Many of the stories that I am going to relate will be experiences that I personally have had under the Scanlon Plan. As you know, I was a machinist at the Lapointe Machine Tool Company and was also very active in the local Steelworkers' Union at that plant. These examples are combined with experience I gained during six and a half years of association with Joe Scanlon in the application of the Plan in the companies represented at this conference.

The Scanlon Plan is difficult to explain because it is not a simple formula. Actually, what we are really going to be talking about is a set of principles or ideals, which I am sure that all of you would agree with, but you might wonder how they can be attained in industry.

A word that is pretty shopworn in industry today is "teamwork," so I am going to spend some time discussing teamwork as I see it. Most of you will agree that at just about all meetings of the many different industrial and management associations there is always a speech given by some company official concerning "teamwork" at his plant. I would venture to say that if you had the opportunity to go back to many of these plants where this so-called teamwork is going on, you might come to the conclusion that it is almost impossible to have teamwork because of the very system under which the employees have to work.

To explain what I am driving at, I want to discuss my own experiences in the plant from which I came and in my later association with Joe Scanlon. Let me give you some examples of what Joe Scanlon used to call the "restraining influences" that are prevalent in most plants today and how they affect "teamwork." One of the more disturbing elements is the approach taken by many companies—that to increase productivity you've got to appeal to the selfish individual. You have to set the individual up in business for himself and make a "free enterpriser" out of him. I was one of those individuals, as an incentive worker, in the plant where I worked. Most incentive or direct workers generally feel that everybody else who isn't a direct worker just hasn't any place in the enterprise. They feel that they are carrying the load of the whole plant on their backs. They think that the so-called indirect (that's the group that the company claims they can't measure) are only in their way, and if these people weren't around things would be much better.

To cite another example, most of us working in plants have always felt that the engineering department never gave any consideration to the tools or the equipment we had to work with when they were developing or designing new products. We always felt that they were living up in their ivory tower and in no way concerned with how their creations had to be made or with the success of the company. At least, that's what we thought. Of course, later on, when I had the opportunity to discover for myself how they felt about their jobs and their relations with us in the plant, it certainly opened my eyes. They weren't too happy when many of us incentive workers were making more money than they were. You can readily see that this "understanding" between engineering and the plant promotes "teamwork"! If any one of us made a mistake in our work and called engineering concerning this mistake, we were very likely to get the answer back: "Follow the print." And when you would plead with them—"Well, it's too late to follow the print, I've already made a mistake!"—it was still, "Follow the print." In some instances it would take nearly a day or two to get some flexibility of agreement as to how you should proceed from there. That's "teamwork" again!

To carry this a step further, there have been cases where the plant will build something that has been engineered by their own engineering department, knowing full well that the product won't work. Yet they will build it anyway and then watch the particular product, or whatever it may be, assembled; and then the comment will go around the plant: "A marvel of engineering, perfect design, best of materials, etc., put together." And then, "Eureka! It doesn't work." What "teamwork"!

Now let's take the next group, the office people. Many factory workers feel that most of the girls in the office knit and the fellows there just smoke cigars. From the factory worker's point of view, office workers make very little contribution to production. Again, I feel this is brought about by the very fact that everybody is confined to the narrow limits of "my job"—what "I," the individual, rather than what "we" in the enterprise, do. There isn't any consideration given to the fact that, as Joe Scanlon always put it, there was never any such thing as an "indirect" or "nonproductive" worker —that everybody working in an enterprise had a contribution to make, whether making the product or servicing it. And if they didn't have a job to do, they ought not to be around. It wasn't until we got under the Scanlon Plan that we recognized the contribution that the engineering, office, and service people could make to whatever we were building.

Another group that has been weakened during the last twenty-five years is the foremen. In many plants, if you go up to a foreman in a particular department and say, "How is this particular worker doing?" he can't give you a quick answer. He has to look up some record to see if that worker is doing so many B hours or whatever it might be, and then he says that the worker is doing a good job. Yet the irony of it is, you may have just left that particular worker, and he has told you that he was spending his time wandering around the plant! In many cases, industry has done more to take away the foreman's job in the last twenty-five years than to aid him to do his job. The fashionable thing to do today seems to be to train him. Now I'm not saying that some training isn't necessary or can't be of benefit, but I think that you ought to concentrate on training him to do his job, not to be a public speaker or a psychiatrist.

But I don't know how you train him to cope with the incentive worker. Looking back to my days in the shop, I can recall that after a very important baseball or football game, we would spend part of the next morning in the plant talking to some fellow workers about what happened at the game. My foreman would walk past me two or three times and then get up enough nerve to come over and say:

"Fred, will you please go to work?" And my usual reply was: "What do you mean, go to work? I'm beating the day's work you set up; I'm beating the standard. It's my money that I'm fooling with. If I want to spend a half an hour talking here, it's my business, not yours. If I wasn't beating the standard, well, then you would have a right to talk to me in such a fashion, but seeing that I am beating what you say is a day's work, then it's my time that I am spending here, whatever I might be discussing." Again, what "teamwork"!

Or, just picture the inspector, who probably is on daywork, being hounded on a particular day by the incentive worker to come over and check his work. The more work the incentive worker does, the more pay he gets; but the more work the inspector does, the same pay he receives—again "teamwork"! Even though they might be "brothers" in the same union, it doesn't seem to make much difference. On many occasions if a machinist on a particular job had spent an hour or more on a job than he actually did, three men might have been able to assemble it in three days rather than spending three weeks because shafts didn't line up, etc. "Teamwork" again, you see! Why, even in many situations the first thing an incentive worker does when he reports to work, on his or her shift, is to find out who the inspector is for that shift. This is because workers generally discover that all human beings are not the same and some inspect differently, so there is no need of doing more work on a part if the inspector will pass the part otherwise. I've actually seen instances where the foreman of one department will mess up the foreman in another department just to make himself look good. "Teamwork" again, you see. It's the old story—"I" seems to be the only important thing; the "we" attitude just doesn't prevail.

Now, I could go on and enumerate literally hundreds of other such problems that tend to make it impossible for people to work together. The industrial engineer, for instance, who comes out to the plant with his stop watch certainly can often do more to control production than to increase it. You may think of this fellow as the expert, but actually the expert is the fellow who is doing the job day-in and day-out. He knows best how it ought to be done. The enemy, to this fellow on incentive, is this industrial engineer with the stop watch; yet they're both working for the same company. "Teamwork" again, you know.

In talking about what the Scanlon Plan is, we need to get away from this "I" concept, and instead, go to "we." If there is to be an incentive in any organization then it ought to be on that product going out the door—more of a better product going out at a lower cost. Certainly, management has its job to do. The union and employees have their jobs to do, and it's how well all of them can do it together which spells the difference between success and failure in the enterprise. What "I" do means very little, but "we" do is very important.

How can you get this "we" environment? Frankly, I think you have to throw out everything that you presently have, whatever it might be in your individual companies, that makes it impossible for people to work together. You have to believe firmly that there is a contribution that people can make who are doing jobs day-in and day-out, that they do have ideas of how the job might be best done. Take the union, for instance. In many firms the only time the union and company get together is when there is trouble. This can be in negotiations; it also can be in the processing of a grievance. These are generally not pleasant associations. However, there is a third area that is left untapped, and that is the area of how to do your job.

You have to use your imagination a bit and realize that there is an area in which a union and a company can get together not as enemies, but as a team, and that is the area of how the product, whatever it might be, is made. We have discovered that we don't know what efficiency is. If a worker knows and understands why he or she is doing something, this can be very important to the outcome of that particular job. Joe Scanlon used to call it "giving people the tools they need to work with."

I would like to emphasize that the Scanlon Plan is not a substitute for leadership; it is something that will thrive on good leadership. The better leadership on the part of management, the better it can work. It means the foreman doing his job, not that of a clerk, but his job as foreman—working with people, planning the work, seeing that the schedules are met, having jobs ready so that when workers complete their job there is another waiting. The foreman under the Scanlon Plan is not a traffic cop trying to chase people out of the rest rooms and walking up and down the floor to make sure they are at their machines. This relationship calls for an entirely new approach —it calls for the foreman to sit down with his people and give them the help that he can by leading them. Under a plan such as this, you cannot have success if the union and the employees want it and the management doesn't want it. And you can't have success if the management wants it and the union and employees don't want it. It takes the combined efforts of both.

This plan doesn't mean turning the plant over to the union. This statement may sound strange, but I don't know any union that wants the responsibilities of running a plant. Under the Scanlon Plan, all we are talking about is providing the opportunity for people to say in an adult society how they think the job might be best done. It's up to management to take it from there. It means workers thinking a little bit more about who gets the job after them and how they might make it easier for them. The Plan means that the older, more experienced worker gives his ideas on how the job ought to be done to the newer worker. It means that the younger worker may be more physically able to help or make his contribution to the older worker. It means management makes decisions on what is good for the company and not on what's good for some personality down in the plant.

This plan doesn't mean giving people a "sense of participation"; workers don't want that. This plan means giving them real participation. You will discover that we have no set formula, that the Plan has worked in these situations because of the desire of both management and labor to get together and mutually solve problems that will help them be more competitive in this industrial society of ours. It means working with your brain instead of your back.

Before getting into a detailed description of what the Scanlon Plan is, however, there is an important group of people in a company that I would like to discuss briefly. This is the accounting department. In my work, during the past eight years, I've been amazed to find how many accounting groups in companies have become so inflexible that they make very little constructive contribution. Rather than accounting servicing the company, it is often true that the company is servicing the accounting group. Why, even in some of these situations it seems to make little difference to the accounting people whether the company was losing or making money. This may seem a little harsh, but what I am driving at is that sometimes when suggestions are made to the accounting people that a change in their system or procedure might help the company, you run into a great deal of resistance. The accountants answer: "We've got a perfect accounting system here, and under no conditions do we want to alter it." The fact that making even minor changes in procedures might help the plant was not important. The thing that seemed most important to these accounting people was "don't disturb our setup."

I share Joe Scanlon's conviction that this particular group can make a contribution that is probably unparalleled in the firm. This is the group that has the records of what is taking place in the firm. But, too often, trying to translate that record into something meaningful, which can be understood by the men and women in the plant, seems to be considered almost impossible. Certainly the jargon used by the accounting people has become quite confusing to the poor foreman out in the plant. I've even heard some foremen jokingly say that they thought a "labor variance" was a new tool to work with, rather than what it really is—excessive costs on a particular product.

Accounting is a very mysterious thing to most union people. Workers just don't understand a "profit." They feel that it can come about or be reduced or eliminated by the manipulations of some accountant. In fact, union people feel in many instances that the company has two sets of books, one for the union and one for the company. If you look at some cases, this is easy to understand. In some of the companies and unions that I have talked with the company began negotiations with the union by discussing how difficult things were and how they were losing money. Workers often feel that the company must have had a huge sum of money to begin with because the company loses money each year they negotiate. Then in these same situations, when the company faces some severe problems and is finally willing to discuss the real facts with its people, company officials are sometimes hurt to find that the people in the shop simply don't believe the accounting figures.

I believe that this is one area where the Scanlon Plan can bring about a significant change of great value to the company, by making it possible for the accounting people to become a real service group to the whole company. On many occasions I can recall Joe Scanlon saying: "If you want people to do something about a problem, give these people the tools to work with." Just saying to a working group, "We are losing money," is not enough. In a sense it is like going to a doctor and saying, "I'm sick, guess what I've got," or going to a lawyer and saying, "I've got a case, guess what it is." The important thing is "Where are we losing money?" Or for that matter, in a particular department, "What cost allowance do we have for this job?" In many cases, the standards set up are meaningless, because in order to get the job the company may have had to cut its price by 10, 20, or 30 per cent. Under conditions such as this you could meet the standard and go broke, so what we are looking for is the best contribution that everybody can make in doing his job. That means accounting people working with these departments to give them the facts and figures, so that the production people might be able to tackle the problem and do something about it.

Just imagine if you can, the tremendous gain from getting all of these different functions in any one company to realize their importance to each other and to develop a willingness to work together. This is real teamwork, as I know it.

We are now ready to get into the two facets of the Scanlon Plan: (1) the measurement or norm, and (2) the actual participation process. In another section of this book the measurement problem will be dealt with in greater detail, but here I want to outline briefly our thinking on the yardsticks that should be used under the Plan.

It was Joe Scanlon's premise that if something is to be effective with work groups, it should be simple and easy to understand. I would venture to say the work we have done in the area of measurements has been quite sloppy. In fact, during the course of a year under the Plan we have depended a great deal on the law of averages to see that the equity of both parties was served under the Plan. If at all possible, we have shied away from profit sharing as such. Our experiences have shown us that profit sharing can be very dangerous. In many situations this comes about because you are tying people down with responsibilities where they have no control. It was always Joe Scanlon's feeling that you can only relate people to problems which they can do something about.

To illustrate this point, several companies have come here to M.I.T. to talk to us about their problems under profit sharing. They all state that when profits were good things went along fine; however, when profits were no longer present, they ran into very serious difficulties with their employees. I think it's quite simple to see why. Under profit sharing a bonus can come about when the company makes a good purchase on materials, or gets a lucky break in some other area that has no real relationship with the operation in the plant. Consequently, in many instances, workers don't know why they got a bonus, so it is reasonable to understand they also don't know why they aren't getting one. The irony of the situation is that some companies have told us, despite the fact that there were no profits for the past few years, they were still paying the "profit-sharing bonus." They indicated that the people felt that it was only deferred wages anyway.

Another difficulty with profit sharing is that payments are too few and far between. A worker has a difficult enough time remembering what happened last week, never mind three or six or twelve months ago. Joe Scanlon always felt that the measurement should be simple and easy to understand, so that when workers received a bonus they knew why they got it, and when they didn't receive a bonus they knew why they didn't get one.

In all of the situations that we have worked with under the Scanlon Plan, the bonus payment has been on a monthly basis. We have generally developed a measurement to fit each individual situation. This meant taking into consideration the peculiarities of the specific plant or company, so that I venture to say that there aren't any two Scanlon measurements exactly alike. Each situation has had to have its own workable measurement. Most of these have involved comparing sales value of production to payroll costs. Now, when I say payroll costs, I'm not just talking about the bargaining unit, I'm talking about the whole plant. Our feeling has been that if you are going to have a plan that's good for the company, everybody ought to be in it, and I mean from the top of the company on down. We have always recommended that you make the team as broad as possible. In fact we like to see everybody from the president of the company to the floor sweeper all in the same plan. I feel that's one of the strengths of the Scanlon Plan.

There is a great deal of mistrust and worry in most situations where you find several plans of remuneration present. Now I'm not just talking about how they might conflict with each other, but about the jealousy that you have when one person is on a more lucrative plan than the other fellow. And if we are talking about real joint participation, then there should only be one plan. I think you can adequately take care of the different skills and wage or salary levels by paying the monthly bonus on a percentage basis. A worker doesn't mind his boss getting a bonus when he is also getting one, but as it so often happens when there is more than one plan in the situation, he gets terribly disturbed when he hears through the grapevine that the boss is getting a bonus and he isn't getting one.

Furthermore, if you are going to have an incentive plan, the incentive ought to be based on more of a better product going out of the shipping room at a lower cost. In your respective companies, you all live or die by that product. We have leaned very strongly towards the dollar measurement, because we have felt that this is the one the worker best understands. The dollar is what he has to support his family on, and it certainly is much more meaningful to him than some far-removed and maybe technically correct standard. We have found that in developing measurements, the more you refine them, the more complicated they get and the more useless they are. The measurements that we have developed have had to be real and live with the times.

We have heard people say, "Take all the variables out of the measurement and once it is set you can live with it without change." I think that is the worst approach you can take. How can you teach people about our free-enterprise system unless they really live under it? Measurements that we have developed have had to change with conditions. Generally we have selected a year's performance as a basis to develop our ratios. The most recent year is always the best, despite the fact that some companies I know of would like to use 1939 as a basis. I think you've got to be realistic. Certainly the most recent year is where you are and is probably the one base period that can work best. Now, it might have to have some adjustments to fit new developments or changes, but nevertheless it is the most realistic base that can be used.

At this point, I am reminded of a Canadian firm which, after reading the *Fortune* article in January, 1950, on the Lapointe experience, proceeded on their own to install the Scanlon Plan. About eight months later, Joe Scanlon got a call from the president of the company, who introduced himself and told him that they had applied the Scanlon Plan. Joe's remarks were as follows: "That's fine. How's it working?" The president of the company indicated that it was working fine; the people had really increased productivity and were doing a good job. Scanlon countered this answer by saying: "Well, that's good, what are you calling me for?" "Well," the president of the company said, "we've got a serious problem." Joe asked, "What is it?" "Well," he replied, "we're getting an increase in productivity, our relationships with our people were never better, but the company's going broke." After some further discussion on the phone, arrangements were made for a team from the company, composed of both management and its people to come down to M.I.T. to meet with Scanlon to discuss their problems. We discovered that after they had read the *Fortune* article, they had developed their measurement just as the article indicated Lapointe did. The only fact that they didn't take into consideration was that the base year they were using for the development of their measurement was one in which the company had incurred severe losses. I merely bring this out to try to get across the point that what works at Lapointe will not necessarily work someplace else. So again I repeat, measurements must be tailored to the individual situation. Certainly in this Canadian company, consideration should have been given to the company's profitability or loss during the base year used. I am sure that if this had been done and discussed with all of the people under the Plan, it would not have been difficult to set a proper ratio or norm.

It is most important, whatever measurement is used, to put all of the cards on the table and hide nothing. You have to stay away from the mumbo-jumbo type of incentive measurements that are now plaguing many plants today. I don't care at what efficiency you think a worker has been performing, if you have accepted it from him day in and day out, that has become a "day's work" to him. To get him to do something different requires a sincere and honest understanding of your joint problem. Whenever we have had to make adjustments in a norm, in the application of the Scanlon Plan, the parties involved have understood why. It was then up to them to decide whether they felt they could do something about it or not.

The development of these measurements reminds me of the first time I was time-studied as a worker. I was new at the job when a young fellow with a board having a stop watch attached to it, came down to my machine one day and indicated to me that he was going to make it possible for me to make more money. He was going to engineer my job for me. Well, since I was a fellow who could never make enough money, this sounded quite appealing. The engineer worked with me for some time and indicated to me that we had a lot in common. He knew I was a union member and said that his dad had belonged to the Sewer Cleaner's Union (or some such union), so after all we were brothers under the skin. Well, after he got through methodizing or engineering my job, he said: "Here's the pitch, because of the laborious type of job that you have, one-tenth out of every hour you can loaf." Well, that sounded pretty good to me, because in those days I was usually quite happy when I was loafing. And he followed it up by saying he knew I had personal needs to take care of, a drink of water, etc., so one-tenth out of every hour I could do that. "Now," he said, "if you will work diligently the other eight-tenths of the hour you can make yourself a 20 per cent bonus." So help me, when he left my machine, I think I was already spending the money! However, the next day when I came to put his theory into practice, I discovered that what I had been doing day in and day out wasn't a day's work according to his computations. Before I could get into this 20 per cent area that he had discussed with me, I had to work about 40 per cent harder.

Well, it's easy to understand that you only get fooled like that once, when you learn to play the game. The time-study engineer then becomes your enemy, and when you start playing the game with him, generally the company comes up on the short end. Because after all, this engineer is dealing with the real expert, the man who is doing the job day in and day out and knows its peculiarities and possibilities. Lo and behold, in many instances, he may come back five or six months later and instead of making 20 per cent bonus, I am making 70 per cent. Then he becomes quite disturbed because I have bastardized his engineering job. I am making too much money. So now an attempt will be made, of course, to re-engineer my job and change the rate. I believe this is quite similar to the Government imposing an excess-profit tax on the company. Let me tell you, workers don't like it any more than do companies.

I bring this point out because we are in the area of measurements. The consultants who come into a firm and say, "Look, there's 20 or 30 per cent cream that you ought to be getting that belongs to the company," is just so much hogwash. If there is that much cream in any of the plants that I'm talking about, then they ought to go out and get it from the workers, if they can. I think you have to be very realistic in applying a measurement. Certainly we have recognized the needs of a company in our work. We have found that a plan is only as good as the ability of both the company and the union to go down the same road together. The Plan just can't work if there are big bonuses to the employees and losses to the company. Conversely, it can't survive if there are huge profits to the company and no bonus to the people for their efforts. So that's why I've said that these measurements have to be realistic. They should be changed when conditions indicate that they should change. In fact, in the Memorandum of Understanding, used in the Scanlon Plan, we say anything that disturbs the equity of either side in the benefits of the plan requires a review of the presently applied ratio to ascertain if any change is necessary.

However, to avoid frequent minor changes, we have strongly recommended in all our work during the last six years, that the union and the company split the benefits of the Plan. Some of the earlier installations, such as Lapointe, were on full participation, in which a 1 per cent increase in productivity meant that a 1 per cent bonus was paid. But now we strongly recommend a split in the benefits, and the one most often used is 75–25, 75 per cent going to the participants under the Plan and 25 per cent going to the company. This means that as the people increase productivity by 4 per cent the company retrieves 1 per cent. Therefore, it is attaining its objective of getting lower labor costs, along with the people getting a fair return for their efforts. By having a split in the benefits, the company does not have to adjust that ratio meticulously for every minor change that comes about.

Earlier I said that most of our measurements have involved the total payroll measured against the sales value of production. We also recommend the use of change in inventory, finished goods, and work in process if the cycle is a long one. These are details that will be discussed in another chapter. But I want to emphasize again that it is very important to have a simple, understandable measurement to apply to any given situation. Even though the measurement is important, it is not nearly so important as the participation part of the Scanlon Plan. If you don't get participation, I don't care what measurement you have or how good it is, it just won't move. One strongly needs the other.

This facet of the Scanlon Plan—participation—is to me the most important. Participation is implemented by setting up what we call production committees and a screening committee. Production committees are established throughout the company—including the office and engineering departments as well as the plant. Each major department has a production committee. Small departments may be grouped together in a single production committee. These committees have representation from both management and labor. Management usually appoints as its member the supervisor of the department or some management person in a decision-making capacity in the company. The union members (or employees where a union does not have bargaining rights) get together and elect someone to represent them on this production committee.

In most instances, we do not have balanced representation on these committees, for there are sometimes as many as six union or employee members meeting with one management member, and this comprises the committee. In other cases, the representation in a production committee may be as small as one management member and one labor member. The function of a production committee is to meet at least once a month (or more often if necessary) to discuss ways and means of eliminating waste, easier and better ways of doing the job, the departmental schedules for that month, and anything else that might pertain to the work going through the department in that month. The committee also processes the suggestions brought in by the union or employee side of the committee. These are often given to them by their fellow employees. It is also the duty of one of the committeemen to record the minutes of their meeting.

The job of the union or employee side of the committee is to convince the management member that the suggestions brought in should be tried or adopted. In many cases, a production committeeman will bring in a person who has given him a suggestion for the meeting, so that the individual can more clearly present his idea to the committee. When the production committee is composed of one union and one management member, it is a very good idea for the union member to bring someone into the meeting with him.

An accurate record is kept of the disposition of each suggestion. Some are accepted and put into effect; others are rejected by the committee because both sides agree that this suggestion is not feasible;

and in some cases there is a difference of opinion because the union or employee side of the committee feels the suggestion has merit and the management member of the committee feels the opposite. None of these suggestions can be thrown out at this level. There is no voting at these production committees on the acceptance or rejection of a suggestion.

Management reserves the right to accept or reject any suggestions that may come in. In fact, in most cases during the early months of the Plan this is the area where we have the most trouble. It has been very difficult for foremen to adjust themselves to receiving ideas from their people on how the job ought to be done. And I want to point out that the foremen are not reluctant about accepting ideas, but they are quite concerned about what their boss might think of them if too many ideas should come from their department. The feeling seems to be that maybe management might think the foreman is not doing his job. Consequently there is a tendency to reject many of the ideas that come in at this level during the early stages of the Plan. It isn't until the company, and that is top management, convinces the foremen or the supervisors that they are being measured differently than in the past. If the Plan is to work, the company will evaluate its lower management group on the basis that the best foreman or supervisor is the one whose department has the most suggestions. This means that this is a department where the people are not afraid to speak up. They are not afraid to participate and to say just how their job might be done easier and better. The old idea that the boss does all the thinking and the employees just do the work is dead.

It is also the responsibility of the management member of the committee to give the other members in advance of the meeting information about any problems that he might have concerning the operation of his department. For example, he might provide information about the production schedule for the month, about the order in which jobs have to go through, or about special bottlenecks, for example. But a production committee should not get involved in grievances, or in anything that might infringe upon the provisions of the collective-bargaining agreement. In many cases the union shop steward may sit in the production-committee meeting held in his area in order to make sure that the functions of the committee are adhered to.

All ideas or suggestions that are accepted and put into effect are contributions to the whole group. No individual award is made for any idea. Also, suggestions are not submitted through a suggestion box but rather are dealt with in an adult fashion by joint-committee discussion of each individual idea. I also want to point out that at the production-committee level we take more pains with a rejected suggestion than one that has been accepted. The reason is that the suggestor whose ideas are accepted and put into effect sees his contribution to the group, but the one whose suggestion has been rejected doesn't know the reason unless he is personally contacted and told why his suggestion was not adopted. You find in most cases that if a person is given the courtesy of a decent answer, he will submit his next good idea to the committee, rather than feeling that proper consideration was not given to his suggestion.

The minutes of the production committee are forwarded as quickly as possible to the screening committee. The composition of the screening committee is generally made up of an equal number of management and union representatives or employees, and its size generally runs between eight and twelve people. On the management side, the representatives should be the top people, and someone like a president or executive vice president of the company chairs the meeting. Other management members are the controller or treasurer, the chief engineer, and the plant manager or plant superintendent. On the union and employee side, the committee is made up of representatives from the areas covered by the production committees. In many situations one, two, or three production committees are included in a group to elect a screening committeeman to represent them from their areas. Also, the president of the local union is a member of the screening committee.

Screening-committee meetings are held at least once a month and their functions are the following: (1) The first order of business is to screen the figures for the previous month and announce the bonus or deficit incurred during that month. (2) The second function of the committee is a discussion by the officials of the company concerning anything that might affect the Plan. Again, I don't mean anything that might conflict with the collective-bargaining agreement but rather the success we are having out in the field with our product, the problems that our sales people are running into in getting new orders, etc. In many instances, the management will bring someone into the meeting who can discuss the serious problems with the committee. (3) The third function of the committee is to screen, through joint discussion, all of the suggestions that have come in from the various production committees. Those which have been accepted and placed into effect at the production-committee level are put into the record; those which have been rejected jointly by the production committee are reviewed; and, finally, decisions are made concerning suggestions on which there occurred a difference of opinion at the production-committee level. All suggestions are judged on their merit and their contribution to all involved, rather than on their effect on some personality down in the plant.

Again, on this committee there isn't any voting on adopting or rejecting a suggestion. Management reserves the right to accept or reject any idea that has been presented. Yet I would venture to say that acceptances of suggestions under the Scanlon Plan has been greater than under any other method. In fact, it is safe to say that most Scanlon Plans that we have installed have a record of better than 90 per cent acceptance on suggestions.

In concluding this discussion on the Scanlon Plan, I repeat that you can see that we have no gimmick. And if management people or union representatives feel that there is a formula or some sort of gimmick that you can just drop into a situation and "presto-chango," things are different, then the Scanlon Plan is not for you. This approach involves a mature relationship. It means treating people like adults and not like children. However, if management and labor can agree jointly on the application of these ideals and principles that I have outlined, I can assure you that they will be entering a new kind of relationship and understanding of each other's problems. And the satisfactions gained from a job well done will exceed the value of whatever employee bonuses and company profits the Plan might generate.

GEORGE P SHULTZ

5 . . . .

Worker Participation
on Production Problems

The idea of participation as a principle of organization has produced exciting and spectacular results. Most recently, for example, Stuart Chase wrote in the January, 1951, issue of *Personnel* about "joint committees which can take output right through the roof by releasing energy and intelligence in the rank and file which hitherto had been bottled up." Other statements by managements, workers, and union leaders have been as extravagant and as enthusiastic.

These testimonials to achievement emphasize the importance of examining further the participation idea. That is the purpose of this article, in which, after brief introductory comment, these five ques-

Author's Note: This article has been adapted by the author from a speech delivered at a conference on "The Frontiers of Personnel Administration," sponsored by the Department of Industrial Engineering of Columbia University. The author wishes to acknowledge the help in the preparation of this article of Joseph N. Scanlon, Charles A. Myers, Douglass V. Brown, and John R. Coleman, all of the Industrial Relations Section, M.I.T.

Reprinted from the November, 1951, issue of *Personnel* by permission of the author and of the publisher, American Management Association, Inc.

tions will be explored: (1) What is the meaning of participation? (2) How were Scanlon's ideas developed?   (3) What are the sources of productivity increases?   (4) What obstacles to success may be identified? and (5) How may the gains from participation be shared?

The idea of participation as a principle of organization is not a new one. It has its roots, after all, in the ageless democratic ideal.   It is expressed in our cultural emphasis on the dignity of the individual and on the value of freely stated opinions before a decision is reached. In the management of our industrial enterprises, also, workers have long been and are now consulted intermittently on immediate production problems.   But the rise and the strength of the American labor movement give testimony that the emphasis in industry has usually been the other way around; on the unquestioned authority and ability of management to make correct and acceptable decisions.   As this philosophy was once stated, "All that a man wants, is to be told what to do and to be paid for doing it."

The idea of worker participation on production problems, of democracy in industry is, basically, then, an old one, yet one that challenges a traditional management philosophy.   Thus, the *fundamental premise* of the participation idea, just the opposite of that quoted above, might be stated in this way: The average worker is *able* to make and, given the right kind of circumstances, *wants* to make important contributions to the solution of production problems.   If you cannot accept this premise, you need consider this question no further.

Joseph N. Scanlon, now on the staff of M.I.T.'s Industrial Relations Section and formerly Director of Research and Engineering for the United Steelworkers of America (C.I.O.), is a leading advocate of *participation* as a basic principle of organization.   With his help, an increasing number of companies and unions are adopting this as a guiding principle in their operations.   The experiences in these cases, which represent a wide variety of industries and of cost and production conditions, will form the basis for our discussion here.   We will be talking exclusively about things that have happened, about facts, about the achievements of people who have worked together.

What Does "Participation" Mean?

At plants where Scanlon's ideas are being followed, people say that they are operating "The Scanlon Plan."   That is a deceptive label. Scanlon offers no rigid formula, no panacea that will solve all your problems, no new production methods to revolutionize your industry. Quite the reverse.   Success from participation stems from hard work and from willingness at all levels of the management organization to face criticism. Using the Scanlon Plan, people learn that solutions to their problems lie within their own organization, not with outside experts. The ideas on production methods and the problems of the business as seen by workers, by foremen, and by top management are laid before members of the organization. The constructive efforts, mental as well as physical, of everyone are solicited. Each individual, then, has the opportunity and feels the obligation to work for the best interests of the group. This is what "participation" means—not only strong criticism of many established practices, but positive and constructive suggestions for improvement.

This is not a limited concept. Workers cannot be expected to "participate on safety but not on scheduling." Many people are talking these days about the importance of "giving workers a sense of participation in the business." They may, for example, distribute copies of the company's annual report to the employees, accompanied, perhaps, by a letter from the president describing one of the company's new products. I am not saying that this is bad; but it is not what I mean here by participation.

The following example will perhaps be useful as an illustration of this point. Not too long ago, a group of about eight workers and their union business agent came to see Scanlon. They were worried people. Their company owned five plants, and the one they worked in was the oldest, the least efficient. As one of them put it, "We've seen these other plants and we know that we're the worst. If business gets bad, we're sure to go." The president of their company had made a number of widely quoted speeches emphasizing the need for giving workers a "sense of participation." These particular workers thought that they had something to contribute, and they had heard that Scanlon talked about "participation," too. Would he help them? Well, he might, but what did they have to contribute? Were they just talking or could they be more specific? Raising this question was like opening the floodgates. The rest of the morning was spent listening to them discuss the mistakes that management made, the unnecessary waste of materials, the possible improvements in methods. The stories were detailed and convincing. Surely they would startle and inspire any company president who talked about participation. They did not inspire this one, though they may have startled him. He stated, in effect, that it was his job to manage this business and that he was paid well to do just that. He was sure the foremen would be glad to get these suggestions, but neither he nor the foremen could discuss them further. After all, he could not give up his management prerogatives.

In order to have participation, then, management must be willing to discuss the real problems of the business, not just the peripheral details of car pools and company picnics. That does not mean that management need give up its decision-making authority to the vote of a group of workers. But it must be willing to discuss relevant problems and decisions and to accept with good grace, at least, suggestions which promise to be productive.

How Scanlon Developed His "Plan"

The story of how this form of participation developed might well begin with Scanlon's background as a cost accountant, industrial engineer and steelworker; but, for our purposes here, we may start with his experience as president of a local union back in 1937. The Steelworkers' Organizing Committee was still really fighting for union recognition in the steel industry. This was a company, however, in which there had been no great difficulty in the organization of the employees. The management didn't vigorously oppose it; they may not have welcomed it enthusiastically, but there were none of the animosities that so frequently grow out of organizing situations.

Wage demands were the order of the day. But the company whose employees Scanlon had organized was in a poor competitive position and was faced with the possibility of liquidation. None of the local people knew what to do about their plight, so they turned naturally to their national office. Clinton S. Golden, an official of the union, tells the story of what happened in this way:[1]

One day a very unusual thing happened. A committee came in from this steel company, bringing with them the president of the company. This committee started to unfold the story. What are we going to do? We don't want to lose our jobs, we like our community, we get along reasonably well with the management. Under this set of conditions, we want the union, we want the wage adjustments; how are we to survive?

"Well," I said, after the situation had been fully discussed, "I haven't got any blueprint to pull out of the drawer and hand you. The union hasn't got any money in the cash box to take out and turn over to you to modify your plant. I think you can be saved, but you will have to save yourselves. There isn't anybody else that can save you. You will have to do it yourself." At the risk of being misunderstood, I continued, "I am a workman— a machinist by trade. I have worked in lots of places and left some in a huff. As far as I know, all the firms I have worked for are still in business and probably some have made a dividend since I left; but I have never

[1] These events were related by Mr. Golden at a conference on the Scanlon Plan held at M.I.T. on April 19-21, 1951.

worked in a place that was so well managed that I didn't think it could be improved. As I have listened to your story, I think this observation applies to your company. Maybe you don't know how poorly it is managed. My advice to you is, go back and try to enlist the interest of every employee in an effort to save your company. I don't care how humble his assignment or position, every employee has something to contribute to this effort. Now you go back, talk it over among yourselves, develop some method for reaching down into the mind of each employee and see what he has got to propose that may possibly result in a reduction of cost or improvement in the quality of the product. See if you can come out in a spirit of teamwork, of working together to save your company."

The sparkplug of this committee was Joe Scanlon. They went back with as little advice as that. And they did develop a way of reaching down, tapping the experience and ideas of every employee, including the common laborer. When they began to get this outpouring of criticism and comment, they began then to find out how much these men knew about the things they were doing, and when these ideas and suggestions were translated into a program of action, they resulted in reduced costs, improved quality of the production, and a solvent company.

As this experience became known in the industry, companies in similar circumstances asked the union to give them that kind of help and cooperation, with the result that Scanlon was called in to the national headquarters of the Steelworkers' Union. His job of showing people the value of their own resources and of the participation of everyone in the organization took him to some 50 companies. This experience served to turn belief into a sure knowledge: there is within the work force an untapped reserve of productivity of major proportions.

The accomplishments of these companies and union members during the adverse years of the late Thirties were spectacular, but they left two major questions unanswered. These companies and workers had developed a cooperative relationship when the very survival of their jobs depended on it; but, without the survival motive, could that kind of relationship be developed? Further, these were companies where efficiency was poor at the start. Suppose this idea were tried in an efficient plant when workers were not afraid of losing their jobs. Could the workers make a significant contribution?

Toward the end of World War II, an opportunity was presented for answering these questions by the experiences of the Adamson Company, a small unionized concern reputedly the most efficient in the storage-tank industry. Mr. Adamson, the company president, had ideas which paralleled Scanlon's. Together with the employees of the firm, they worked out a method for sharing the gains from productivity increases (a method which officials of the War Labor Board accepted as paying bonuses *only* to compensate for increases in productivity). They set up "production committees" of management and worker representatives and Adamson himself presided over a "screening committee" which discussed and decided on major policy questions. This was a company, then, which had made a profit even in 1932, which paid high wage rates, and which was acknowledged "the best" from the standpoint of efficiency. During the first year of participation under the Scanlon Plan, the workers' average bonus (productivity increase) was 41 per cent. According to Adamson, he made two and a half times the profit he would have made had he remained at the previous level of productivity.[2]

Following this experience at the Adamson Company, other companies and unions have successfully applied this principle of participation. The case of the Lapointe Machine Tool Company, described in the January, 1950, issue of *Fortune*, is probably the most widely publicized; but the Scanlon Plan is now operating in such diverse industries as furniture, silverware, steel fabricating, printing, rubber processing, corrugated paper containers, and radio and television. The companies range in size from 60 employees to 5000 and include multiplant as well as single-plant concerns. Close contact with these cases provides convincing evidence that the essential condition for success is not survival, not big bonus money, certainly not "inefficient" plants, but willingness and desire to have all members of the organization participate in solving its problems.

What Are the Sources of Productivity Increases?

Are people working that much harder? Are these new ideas from the work force as revolutionary as all that? These are questions quite naturally raised by everyone who hears of results like those achieved at Adamson and Lapointe. They are good questions and deserve a careful answer. People may not be working harder, but they are certainly working more effectively. Conscious restriction of output by individuals and groups gradually disappears, a helping hand is offered when the going is tough, and workers no longer take their major satisfaction from fooling the boss and killing time in the washroom. New ideas contributed by workers, often simple and "obvious" once they have been presented, are also an important source of productivity

---

[2] For more information on this case, see Joseph N. Scanlon, "Adamson and His Profit-Sharing Plan," *AMA Production Series No. 172*, 1947, pp. 10–12, and John Chamberlain, "Every Man a Capitalist," *Life*, December 23, 1946.

gains. After all, the worker is *much* closer to his job than anyone else, so he naturally has ideas of his own about it. But it would be a mistake to assume this to be a complete accounting. At least four other ways in which productivity is improved can be identified. I would like to give you an illustration of each one, taken from the experience of a printing company.

1. *Old ideas that have previously been impossible to implement become readily acceptable after coming forth as worker suggestions.* The following is an example:

One of the pressroom employees pointed out that waste paper was now being crumpled up and thrown in a basket in preparation for salvage. Everyone conceded that, if this paper could be salvaged in flat form, its value would be much higher. Management had been aware of this possible saving but had been unable to enlist the cooperation of the employees in keeping the stock flat. A committee member pointed out the reason for the lack of cooperation: workers felt the foreman was trying to check on them to see how much paper they wasted. Consequently, through various subterfuges they made it impossible for him to police his system. With the suggestion and impetus coming from the employees themselves, however, there was no trouble in getting the waste paper placed in flat form on pallets located at appropriate places in the pressroom.

2. *When management has an idea or a program for plant improvements, it can take them to the people affected and ask for further suggestions and comments.* The result is a better program and a more acceptable program as well. Here is an example.

In the process of binding a sewed book, a group of loosely sewed sixteen or thirty-two page "signatures" must be brought together in stiff form and rounded in the back as preparation for putting on the cover of the book. This stiffening is provided by the application of glue to the back of the book, and it must dry at least one hour before the backing machine is used. For many years the gluers had placed their work on movable tables which were then pushed to the backing machine. Before the installation of the participation plan, the company's planning department had decided that these tables should be replaced by a series of fixed conveyors. This conveyor system was explained to the superintendent and foreman involved, and a blueprint of the proposed conveyor system was placed on the bulletin board in the department. However, the employees were told by the foreman that they were not allowed to look at this bulletin board except on their own time—that is, during the lunch hour. They were not told what the blueprint was all about, and they did not understand that it involved a drastic change in the layout of their workplace.

During the holiday of Christmas week, 1948, the conveyor was installed. The employees, several of whom had worked for the company for 20 to 25 years, were amazed when they came back from vacation and found their workplace totally changed. They did not like the conveyors from the moment they saw them, and when the lack of the flexibility in the conveyor system produced confusion and frustration for management, the employees were delighted. They drew a large X on the window and, when asked what this X meant, replied, "It marks the spot." "What spot?" "The spot where the conveyor goes out!"

Before the conveyor was installed, production in the department had been averaging over 500 books per hour per work team and, in some months, had even exceeded 600 books. During the first 10 months of 1949, production dropped to an average of about 450 books per hour per team and in some months went below 400 which was a new low for the department. The employees in the bindery brought the inadequacies of this conveyor system first before their production committee and then before the screening committee. The planning department tried hard to defend its baby. A group from the screening committee, including the plant manager, however, looked at the operation and decided unanimously that the conveyor system did not provide the conditions under which high production could be achieved.

Essentially, the conveyor system would work well only when an ideal set of scheduling conditions were possible, and the planning department agreed that such ideal conditions were the exception rather than the rule. The screening committee ordered the conveyors removed, and the department went back to the old system. On the second week after going back to the old system production was back up to 525 books per hour per team and has since been maintained at approximately that level.

In contrast to this experience is the installation of a conveyor system after the plan had been in operation for two months. As in the former case the planning department had an idea for the rearrangement of the machines and the use of a conveyor to facilitate certain transport problems. In this case a blueprint was made and posted on the bulletin board, but the employees stated that they could not read the blueprint and that, therefore, they could make very few, if any, suggestions about the proposed plan. Consequently, a small-scale model or templet of what the layout would look like under the new plan was placed at a central location in the department. The employees still, however, made practically no suggestions about the new plan.

One afternoon a member of the planning group happened to be in the department and started discussing the proposed layout with a few of the employees. After he had criticized the proposal in a number of respects, a great many comments were made both by the foreman and by the employees. These comments were gathered together and a production committee meeting was held, attended by the industrial engineer responsible for the proposal. At this meeting the employees and the foreman joined together in strenuous criticism of the conveyor part of the plan. After about two and one-half hours' discussion, the production committee agreed that the rearrangement of the machines would be beneficial but wanted the engineer to reconsider several aspects of the conveyor system.

About a week later, another meeting was held, and the production committee agreed to a modified version of the conveyor system, with the understanding that it would be installed in such a manner that they could make changes fairly easily. Subsequently, the production committee did make several important changes, especially in the manning of the new system. The drastic revision in the department layout and the revised conveyor system are now accepted as an improvement by the workers and the foremen concerned and the productivity of the department has been increased by about 20 per cent.

3. *When a particular problem arises of concern either to one department or to the plant as a whole, it is possible to communicate the real nature of the problem to the people involved.* Given such a sense of direction, individual and group efforts often provide important contributions to an effective solution. The following is an example.

The long-term problem in the press room was loss of work to outside manufacturers who, because of their clearly superior equipment, could presumably turn out the work more cheaply than it could be done at the plant on old flatbed presses. One of the chief losses was the approximately two million workbooks a year contracted for by an outside press. With their own bread and butter at stake, the pressroom committee investigated the relative cost of doing the work at the plant as against sending it outside. They found that the outside price was $15.90 per hundred for a particular order and that the planning department figured the cost of doing this job in the plant was $21.55 per hundred, a differential of $5.65 for each 100 workbooks. Using these figures as a point of reference, the production committee showed management how the plant costs could be brought down to $17.65 per hundred. This tremendous saving was the result of two factors: (1) the elimination of unnecessary operations, and (2) reductions in the estimated time requirement on the operations that were performed. By further investigation into other books of this type, the production committee found that certain administrative costs that were properly incurred by the company were not allocated to outside work. Further, extra costs incurred by the company as a result of sending the work outside (for example, trucking cost, and extra paper used by the outside plant) were not counted at all when considering the outside bid. Finally, it was found that the reduction of in-plant overhead cost per unit resulting from the possible increased volume was not being considered. When all these factors were taken into consideration, it was found that a specific 50,000 workbook order could be produced at the plant for 50¢ per hundred cheaper than it could be printed outside—a figure 28 per cent under management's original cost estimate. This was just the first specific order of a large number which could be examined carefully by the management in close collaboration with the production committees and which might be returned to the plant.

4. *Management tends to improve in the performance of its own functions.* There are two reasons behind that improvement. In the first place, individuals in the management hierarchy are put more clearly "on the spot." Repeated mistakes get a thorough airing, with the result that supervisors are kept on the alert. Second, management gains much more reliable information about the way the plant is actually operating. Thus, it is able to improve the performance of its functions because it has more and better information upon which to base its actions. Here is an example:

One of the departmental production committee's most vigorously pressed suggestions concerned the scheduling of jobs. Workers complained that they often set up their equipment as scheduled, only to find that the particular paper needed for that job was not yet on hand. Though paper for other jobs was apparently available, they could not make a switch since setup time was generally great. This complaint involved people outside the department, however, so the production committee could do little about it themselves. They passed it on to the top screening committee, a group which included the company president.

The head of the scheduling department, of course, felt particularly concerned with this complaint, and so he did some "homework" in preparation for the meeting. For each job, the worker turns in to the scheduling department a time slip, on which is tabulated the total elapsed hours in terms of "running time," "delays," and so on. The department head examined his file of these slips thoroughly and found that there was actually very little delay due to "insufficient paper." When the question came up in the meeting, he triumphantly produced these "facts" and discounted the complaint as of minor importance. This disclosure was greeted with an embarrassed silence. After a long half-minute, one of the workers spoke up: "Those time slips are way off. We fill them out. We were told by the foreman that he would get in trouble if we showed that delay time, so we usually added it to the running time. We've been doing it that way for years. We had no idea you were using the slips as a basis for planning."

Further discussion brought out that the schedulers were using the time slips, not just as a check on coordination between paper storage and production departments, but also as a basis for calculating the running times on different types of jobs. Now, with a newly reliable source of information, the scheduling department is able to work much more effectively.

The examples which we have examined here will, it is hoped, serve to illustrate the variety of ways in which productivity may be increased under a "participation" plan. They should serve as well to point up more clearly the meaning of "participation" and the powerful potential of this idea. Some of the things that have happened in Scanlon Plan situations have been genuinely dramatic; many more have been unspectacular and even commonplace to an outsider—but every one of those events has been representative of the tapping of resources which management, by and large, has neglected in past years.

Two Obstacles to Success

None of us, I am sure, will conclude that these results have been effortlessly achieved or that the installation of this "plan" proceeds without obstacles and problems. The two questions most probably in the reader's mind now are, in fact, "How can individual workers be persuaded to adopt the constructive attitude indicated by the preceding examples?" and "How can the union be induced to cooperate so wholeheartedly with management?" Experience indicates that these two problems, while significant, may not be so great as management initially assumes. Where management accepted the union without reservation and understood the union's objectives and way of operating, the union has cooperated and grown stronger in the process. The parties have cooperated on problems of productivity, while still continuing to bargain collectively over wages, hours, and working conditions. And, as they found their ideas welcomed and accepted, workers have gradually assumed a more and more responsible attitude toward production problems. Even in a plant with eight different unions representing the work force, these "union" and "worker" obstacles have not been insurmountable.

But two other obstacles, often overlooked by management, have been most troublesome. These obstacles are (1) the initial loss of prestige and consequent opposition of middle and lower management people and (2) the inability of the organization to make important decisions on an explicit basis.

1. Meeting Resistance of Supervisors

Successful installation of this plan reorients completely the job of supervision. Whereas foremen and superintendents may have previously been accustomed to complete authority over technical production decisions, those decisions must now be made after consultation with the employees. In many cases, such consultation shows up previous practices as ill-considered at best and just plain stupid at worst. That kind of dramatic exposition, often not put too diplomatically by the employee, may undermine the personal security of line management people. Many of them try initially to suppress the efforts of the production committees, and only forceful and prompt action by top management makes the continuance of committee efforts possible. Others react with lengthy rationalization, explaining why none of the employees' suggestions can be carried out or asserting that the ideas have been in their minds a long time, but that the employees would not cooperate in carrying them out.

Clearly identified, this obstacle can be dealt with effectively. First of all, *top management must be unambiguously committed to the operation of this plan.* Foremen must not be allowed to retaliate against members of departmental production committees or to break up meetings of these committees. Where sabotage of the Plan is open, management must be prepared to fire the foreman as a last resort. Second, and more important in the long run, top management must use incidents where friction between workers and supervisors occurs as an opportunity for re-orienting the supervisor in his attitude toward his job. This educational approach has its positive side as well. When a department presents an unusual number of good suggestions, top management might well commend the foreman or, at the very least, not criticize him for "being shown up by the workers."

Finally, if initial difficulties can be surmounted, successful operation of the plan gives to the supervisory force a constantly accumulating number of convincing experiences. They see things happen that seemed impossible under the old circumstances. They come to know their people better and are accepted by their people as a member of a team with a common goal. Their contribution as coordinator and organizer of the work is more fully appreciated. In short, they find that the Plan gives to them a superior method of solving their daily production problems.

2. "Finding the Boss"

Many organizations have developed the habit of postponing decisions wherever that is possible. Rather than decide the issue and risk being proved wrong, management may often decide not to decide, to await further developments. But by the time these developments have occurred, there is no decision left to make: there is only one alternative. This implicit type of decision-making, more widespread than we might care to admit, is not consistent with successful operation of the plan. Suggestions pour in, routines are questioned, issues are laid out on the table where all can see them. If no action is taken, dissatisfaction grows and the people rapidly lose their interest. Why should I make suggestions, they say, if nothing is done about them? This difficulty in "finding the boss" is usually of special significance in multiplant operations, where all or most authority may lie beyond the bounds of the particular plant.

This does not mean that management must always go along with the ideas of the work force. In many instances, the question is one of judgment, and the boss must be the judge. As one worker put it, "That's really what we're paying him for." What the work force does demand is an opportunity to be heard. Given that opportunity, they want decision, not procrastination. In other words, the organization must have a boss, but the boss must be accessible to the organization.

Sharing of the Gains

Continuing results cannot be expected without some method for a sharing of the gains from increased productivity. A monetary incentive is, of course, of real importance, especially in situations where survival is not in question. But that is not the only reason for attaching a financial incentive to this plan. In addition to the positive-incentive aspect of monetary payment, the need for some *quid pro quo* is strong. As one worker put it, "I'm too old to be chasing a carrot around, but, damn it, if we do something that's worth something, we want to be paid for it." Second, the existence of a measurement of productivity gives the workers a sense of direction and accomplishment which they could not otherwise get. They know, in other words, what is "par" for this course and whether or not they have fallen short of or improved on this standard of accomplishment. Finally, discussion of changes in the measure of productivity often illuminates the problems of the business dramatically. If productivity is down, something will be learned by finding out why it is down. Knowing why, workers do not lose faith and interest as a result of periods in which no bonus is paid. Changed or difficult circumstances are discovered and treated explicitly. Thus, discussions can be a rich source of new ideas, facilitating necessary adjustments.

What kind of measurement should be used? Generally speaking, incentives such as profit sharing are too broad. The measure should be related more closely to the productivity of the participating group. Only on the basis of the group's efforts should it be rewarded—not on the basis of fortuitous price changes or inventory speculations. This goal has led, wherever possible, to the use of a ratio relating the payroll of the group to the sales value of production (sales revenue plus or minus real changes in inventories of finished goods). A bonus is paid when, with a given payroll, the group produces more than the "norm" production value. This method does not, of course, give an exact and scientific measure of productivity. *There is no such measure.* It does give, however, a rule of thumb that is roughly accurate and is easily understandable. Members of the participating group know what went into the original calculation, and so, if basic conditions change, they will agree to revise the norm. For example, changes can be made in the event of revisions of product prices, basic wage rates, or major machine installations. Experience with such rough measurements and with changes for good and proper reasons has been uniformly successful. Thus the "formula" works, not because it is precise and invulnerable but because the parties approach the problem of sharing the gains with understanding, good faith, and mutual trust.

Conclusion

Our discussion here has centered on the tangible results of real participation. We have talked about bonus payments and about higher profits. We have touched on the difficulties of getting started and on the fruits of success, in terms of specific suggestions and accomplishments. If you were to visit one of these "participating" plants, to talk with workers and union and management officials, I am sure you would be told about those achievements. But, as you left the plant, I doubt that you would be thinking of the tangible gains. Your thoughts would be focused, rather, on the enthusiasm with which your questions had been greeted, on the knowledge of the business displayed throughout the plant, and on the pride with which accomplishments were described. You would say to yourself, "Here are people at work, not resentful and suspicious, not just here because they have to earn their living. They are enjoying their work. They are participating."

ELBRIDGE S. PUCKETT

6 . . . .

Measuring Performance under the Scanlon Plan

Most people who are interested in exploring the Scanlon Plan start with the belief that the "ratio" is a unique and central focal point and that it is a mysterious tool or gimmick which accomplishes miracles. Perhaps this is a carry-over from the thinking underlying individual incentive systems where the focus of attention and emotion naturally centers on the standard itself. However, Joe Scanlon was not suggesting as a substitute for piecework simply a new method of measuring performance. He was talking of something much broader in scope— a new communication process, a new approach to solving the never-ending problems that face business and industrial organizations; in short, a new relationship among people at work.

The purpose of this paper is to place the Scanlon Plan ratio in proper perspective to these broader aspects. We shall consider (1) how the measurement is developed and how it works, (2) the basic principles involved in such a measurement as compared with other standards, and (3) the relationship of the measurement to communication and cooperation in the productive unit.

In approaching this subject it must be remembered that Scanlon's guiding rules for achieving a better utilization of the work force (and hereafter the term "work force" is used in the broadest possible sense —to include all employees of the company from top management on down) was to eliminate the "restraining influences" which kept people from entering fully into the productive effort and achieving the satisfaction that can come only from pride of achievement. The measuring device of piecework incentives is only one, although a very important one, of these restraining influences. Hence the underlying theme of this discussion is that the measurement is an important ingredient of successful application of the Scanlon Plan, but no matter how "good" the measurement is, it can never be a substitute for good management, leadership, willingness to share problems and listen to suggestions, and sincere willingness and desire on the part of all concerned to do the job better than ever before.

The ratio discussed in the following section is not the only type that has been used. In each application the measurement has been tailored to meet the needs of that situation. It has been our experience that where there is a sincere desire to develop a more creative and rewarding relationship, some equitable and understandable measure of performance can be found.

The Measurement

The Scanlon Plan ratio basically is a very simple concept which measures in some historical period the relationship between total payroll in a particular productive unit and the sales value of what was produced by that payroll. Once this relationship has been established, for any month under the Plan when the labor costs are below this norm, the difference between the norm payroll and the actual payroll constitutes the bonus pool. Before the actual payment of the bonus, however, some percentage of the bonus pool is usually set aside in the reserve to protect the company against possible deficit months, in which the actual payroll exceeds the norm. In many cases 25 per cent of the bonus pool has been more than adequate to protect the company, but this figure may vary from one situation to another. After setting aside the reserve the balance is split, with 25 per cent going to the company and 75 per cent being paid out in an immediate cash bonus to participants in the Plan. The 25–75 split has become common practice in recent years, but is not universal. In two of the earliest applications participants in the Plan shared 100 per cent of the labor savings.

The bonus is paid to individuals as a per cent of their participating payroll, which differs from the actual payroll by vacation (and sometimes holiday pay), probationary payroll, and time not worked by salaried employees. Some explanation of these exclusions may be in order. The bonus is not paid on vacation pay for the reason that only actual effort in the production process should be remunerated through the bonus system. The same principle applies with respect to salaried employees whose pay goes on when they take time off for personal reasons. Probationary payroll is that pay for new employees who are considered not fully trained or full participating factors in the organization. The probationary period varies from company to company but often follows the same probationary period which has been used by the company in previous employment policy. Most unions prefer that new people start participating as soon as possible, particularly if skill is not a major factor and if the time necessary for the probationary worker to get into effective production is short.

The reserve is set up on a yearly basis, as the ratio usually reflects the fluctuations over the seasons of the year. At the end of the Scanlon Plan year (which may or may not be a calendar year), if the portion that has been set aside in the bonus months exceeds the total deficits incurred, the balance is paid out in the same way as a monthly bonus. The company takes 25 per cent of the reserve pool, and the remaining 75 per cent is paid out to the workers in the usual way. If at the end of the year the total deficits exceed the portion set aside in the reserve, the company absorbs the deficits and the next year starts on its own.

Perhaps the development and operation of the ratio can best be understood by referring to a specific example. Table 1 shows the figures which made up the ratio which was developed for one company for the calendar year 1956. The method used in developing the ratio in this example is not the only method that has been used, but it is the most common method and one which is very desirable if at all practical within the particular accounting system.

The figures used include Net Sales, Change in Inventory, and Total Payroll for everyone involved in this company. The sales figures are Net Sales after Returns, Allowances, and Freight-out. Using this net figure provides a measure of the net effectiveness of the entire productive unit. If, on the other hand, Gross Sales were used, a bonus could be paid on merchandise or on products which were returned for faulty workmanship. Also Freight-out is a figure which varies in relation to the distance of the buyer and has no relationship to the productivity of the plant's operation.

Table 1. Development of Ratio

1956	Net Sales (1)	Changes in Inventory (In Process and Finished Goods) (2)	Sales Value of Production (3)	Factory Payroll (4)	Office and Salary (5)	Reserve for Vacations and Holidays (6)	Total Adjusted Payroll (7)	Ratio of 7 to 3 (7) ÷ (3)
January	$ 846,349	$ 15,365	$ 861,714	$ 185,796	$ 79,627	$ 12,402	$ 277,825	32.2
February	855,555	78,532	934,087	204,949	87,836	12,402	305,187	32.7
March	795,326	−9,856	785,470	194,916	83,535	12,402	290,853	37.0
April	682,540	11,363	693,903	200,547	85,949	12,402	298,898	43.1
May	754,430	61,337	815,767	216,148	92,635	12,402	321,185	39.4
June	863,115	−6,542	856,573	225,032	96,442	12,402	333,876	39.0
July	462,867	20,853	483,720	132,861	56,941	12,402	202,204	41.8
August	921,173	12,624	933,797	218,231	93,527	12,402	324,160	34.7
September	950,161	−3,009	947,152	217,834	93,357	12,402	323,593	34.2
October	851,333	8,751	860,084	239,100	102,471	12,402	353,973	41.2
November	826,551	17,883	844,434	254,094	108,898	12,402	375,394	44.4
December	703,158	10,767	713,925	210,704	90,301	12,402	313,407	43.9
	$9,512,558	$218,068	$9,730,626	$2,500,212	$1,071,519	$148,824	$3,720,555	38.2

Net Sales are adjusted for the Changes in Inventory to relate the bonus as closely as possible to the period in which it is earned. Where the accounting system permits, the Change in Inventory should involve only the change in Work in Process and Finished Goods. Changes in Raw Stock or Materials which have not gone into process have no relationship to production. Usually inventories are valued at "cost," which means that the Plan does not get full credit for production in inventory until it is sold. This provides a strong incentive to ship the product as soon as possible. In some cases inventory has been valued at sales prices where seasonal market conditions cause wide divergence between production and sales and where inventory cost is a small percentage of sales value. On the other hand, there are a few cases where a fast production cycle keeps inventory changes slight so that there is no need for an inventory adjustment.

Adding or subtracting the Change in Inventory from Net Sales results in what is loosely termed the Sales Value of Production. This is the measure of what was produced during the period and can be found in Column 3 in Table 1.

The payroll included in the Plan involves the gross pay of everyone who is to participate in the Plan. In a single-plant company it is desirable to include everyone from the management on down. In a multiplant situation it has often been found desirable to include all people working at the geographical location of the plant. In some cases salesmen are included in the Plan, and in all cases office people who service the sales department participate in the Plan with the office group.

Payrolls are often divided into the factory payroll and the office and salary payroll. The screening committee is usually interested in following the relationship between the Factory Payroll and the Total Payroll. The Factory Payroll involves gross pay (including overtime, shift premiums, and any bonuses or incentive payments received). In the same fashion the Office and Salary Payroll involves gross pay (including any bonuses or premiums). Vacation and holiday expenses are usually pulled out of the month in which they are paid, and each month is assessed with one-twelfth of the annual total, so that no one month bears a disproportionate share of the vacation or holiday burden.

Breaking the figures down in this fashion and assembling them in Table 1 we find that in the month of January, 1956, Net Sales were $846,349 and the Inventory Change $15,365. Adding the increase in Inventory to the Net Sales gives a value of production for the month of $861,714. To produce this sales value required a Factory Payroll of $185,796 and an Office and Salary Payroll of $79,627. Adding to this the January share of the vacation and holiday expense of $12,402 results in a Total Adjusted Payroll of $277,825. Now if we divide the Total Payroll by the Sales Value of Production we find that every dollar of sales costs 32.2 cents in our labor bill. Following the same procedure for each of the twelve months of 1956 we find that the labor ratio varies between 32.2 per cent and 44.4 per cent, for the month of December. These variations are important, for the ratio is not simply a mathematical formula but is an average which is made up of high-labor-cost months and low-labor-cost months. The magnitude of these variations gives us some guide as to the percentage of the bonus pool which may be reserved to protect the company against possible deficits resulting in the high-labor-cost months. To arrive at the ratio for the year 1956, the Total Payroll of $3,720,555 is divided by the total Sales Value of Production of $9,730,626, which produces a ratio of 38.2 per cent.

Assuming that the company and union in our example put the Plan into effect in January, 1957, we can calculate the first month's bonus as shown in Table 2. From Gross Sales are subtracted Freight-out and Sales Returns and Allowances to arrive at Net Sales. In this month we produced more than was sold and the Inventory increased $67,076, which is added to Net Sales to arrive at the Sales Value of Production. The Allowed Payroll, or that payroll which would have resulted on the average in the base period, is 38.2 per cent of $950,123, or $362,947. Adding our Factory Payroll, Office and Salary Payroll, and Vacation and Holiday Reserve, we arrive at an Actual Payroll of $307,650 which is subtracted from the Allowed Payroll generating a Bonus Pool of labor savings of $55,297.

Twenty-five per cent of the Bonus Pool is set aside in the Reserve, and this amount is added to the Reserve Account at the bottom of the table. It can be seen in the Reserve Account that of the $13,824, 75 per cent is the employees' equity and 25 per cent is retained by the company. After subtracting the Reserve, the balance is shared 25 per cent by the company and 75 per cent by the employees. The employees' share ($31,105) is distributed by dividing that amount by the Participating Payroll of $295,248 yielding a bonus per cent of 10.5 per cent for the month. The Participating Payroll in this case equals the Total Payroll minus the Vacation and Holiday Reserve, assuming that there were no probationary employees and no time lost by salaried people. In this month each employee participating in the Plan would receive 10.5 per cent of his gross pay for the month. Bonus must be paid on overtime as required by the Fair Labor Standards Act.

Before applying the ratio resulting in a particular situation it may be

Table 2. Calculating the Bonus

Scanlon Plan—January, 1957

Gross Sales		$898,780
Less Freight-out	$ 12,268	
Less Sales Returns	3,465	15,733
Net Sales		$883,047
Plus Increase in Inventory		67,076
Sales Value of Production		$950,123
Allowed Payroll (38.2% of $950,123		362,947
Actual Payroll:		
Factory Payroll	$206,674	
Office and Salary Payroll	88,574	
Reserve for Vacations and Holidays	12,402	307,650
Bonus Pool		$ 55,297
Reserve for Deficit Months (25%)		13,824
Bonus Balance		$ 41,473
Company Share (25%)		10,368
Employee Share (75%)		$ 31,105
Bonus Paid as % of Participating Payroll*		10.5%
(i.e., $31,105 ÷ $295,248)		

Status of Reserve: January 31, 1957

	Total Reserve	Employee Share (75%)	Company Share (25%)
Beginning Balance	$———	$———	$———
Added this Month	13,824	10,368	3,456
Ending Balance	$13,824	$10,368	$ 3,456

* Participating Payroll equals Total Payroll minus Vacation and Holiday Reserve (i.e., $307,650 − $12,402).

necessary to adjust for substantial changes in conditions since the base period. Looking back over the labor-cost experience for five or ten years can give a great deal of guidance as to the problems that the ratio may face. However, past experience often indicates that changes wash out and the ratio is quite stable from year to year. This is not to say that ten years of stability cannot be vastly altered by basic changes in products or processes.

In the same manner the ratio may require adjustment at any time after the Plan has been in operation. The accounting mechanics of adjusting the ratio are relatively simple. The basic principle to be followed is to project the new conditions back to the base period and determine what effect they would have had on the ratio.

Price changes are easily administered by adjusting Net Sales in the base period for the percentage increase or decrease in prices. After changing the Net Sales, a new ratio is then computed. Where price increases vary in per cent among different product lines, the percentage change in prices can be weighted by the per cent of the total sales mix that is involved with each percentage price increase.

Wage changes may be adjusted in similar fashion. The percentage increase is applied to the base period payroll of the group affected. Product mix may be adjusted on the basis of the change in labor content. To illustrate with an example assuming that product A is 50 per cent and product B is 50 per cent of the total sales mix and that each dollar of product A costs in the base period 10 cents for labor and each dollar of product B costs 20 cents for labor. If product B shifts to 60 per cent of the total mix and product A to 40 per cent, the adjustment may be as follows:

Base Period:

Labor in product A $= .10(.50) = .05$ (Sales Value of Production)
Labor in product B $= .20(.50) = \underline{.10}$ (Sales Value of Production)

Total labor content $= .15$ (Sales Value of Production)

After Shift in Product Mix:

Labor in product A $= .10(.40) = .04$ (Sales Value of Production)
Labor in product B $= .20(.60) = \underline{.12}$ (Sales Value of Production)

Total labor content $= .16$ (Sales Value of Production)

The above analysis indicates the total labor content has increased 1 per cent of the Sales Value of Production and the ratio may be adjusted by that per cent.

Technological changes involving substantial changes in equipment or processes may be adjusted in the ratio by determining the labor which is relieved for other duties as a result of the technological change and reducing the base-period payroll by this amount.

One final word of caution concerns the profitability of the firm during the base period. Clearly, a company cannot judiciously freeze into the future a cost structure that produced a loss. Firms that have faced this situation have found that workers respond readily to an adjustment in the ratio that will get the company out of the red if the facts are fully laid on the table. Once workers have confidence in the integrity of the company's figures, they need no additional education to apprise them of the relationship between their job security and the company's ability to stay in business.

In such situations, experience suggests that it is much healthier to adjust the ratio to a break-even basis than to attempt to protect the company by deepening the split in labor savings. Laying the facts on the table and adjusting the ratio to a level which must be attained to insure the health of the enterprise focus attention on the job that must be done and illustrate one of the central reasons why the union perhaps has had difficulty in negotiations and why job security has been tenuous; namely, labor costs are out of line with competition. Also, there is a sense of equity and sharing in setting the break-even point of the Plan at a level similar to that of the company, so that the company and employees begin to share in improvements at roughly the same point.

Principles Underlying This Measurement

The first principle underlying the Scanlon Plan ratio is that it directs itself to the group rather than the individual. This puts everyone on the same team and promotes cooperation rather than competition. Joe Scanlon used to say that most companies have too much competition on the outside to foster competition from within. Attention is focused on the performance of the group, which in the final analysis is what we live and die by. The growing importance of indirect and office workers in American industry emphasizes the need to include this group in any measurement of performance as well as the need for providing this group with an incentive to do a better job.

A principle that is often overlooked yet one which can be most significant is the educational value of focusing attention on variables which are of critical importance to the firm. When there is an adverse shift in product mix, or a decline in sales, or a competitive-pricing problem, employees immediately feel the effects, attempt to isolate the reasons, and attempt to conquer the problem. Merely understanding the cause makes it much easier to weather a rough storm —much easier than when the worker thought all adversity started with a bum decision by management. Many companies spend tremendous sums today to educate their employees in the economics of the free-enterprise system. What better education can the workers get than by living, feeling, and working with the most basic problems of the particular enterprise of which they are a part?

The use of sales figures rather than some physical measure is an important ingredient in regard to employee understanding of the total picture. In highly competitive situations, workers have become so sensitive to the relationship between costs and prices that occasionally they have taken the lead in suggesting that the company lower prices to bring in more work. When the worker learns of the many problems imposed on the company by external forces, it is amazing what he can do in terms of adjusting to these problems and making the most of a difficult situation.

Limiting the measurement to labor costs ties the work force to an area over which they have a reasonable amount of control. Under profit sharing, every expense item from advertising and travel expenses to capital-equipment expenditures is subjected to scrutiny by employees. The result may be that valuable time is spent by production people questioning decisions completely outside their area of control, and much disenchantment may result from a lack of understanding of such decisions or lack of agreement. Under the Scanlon Plan there are also many uncontrollable factors which may influence bonus opportunity such as faulty materials and declining sales volume. However, such factors are always being dealt with by the production unit and are readily understood, and in a sense they present the challenges which must be dealt with explicitly if the enterprise is to be successful.

One principle underlying the Scanlon Plan ratio that is of vital importance is that the "standard" is set by the people themselves. From the worker's viewpoint this is quite different from having some engineer or some outsider come in and say what ought to be the standard. Good, bad, or indifferent, whatever the work force did in a representative base period is the bogie that they have to beat. The company achieves its goal of lower labor costs through the split in the benefits of the plan. Such a standard leaves little room for argument about what is "fair" but focuses attention on what can be done to improve.

Adjustments that have been made in the ratio have not been related to performance or earnings, but only to changes in external conditions which distort the ratio as a measure of performance. Thus there is less incentive to control production to "protect the standard." It is imperative, of course, that management has entered into the Scanlon Plan relationship with a sincerity that alleviates fears concerning arbitrary management action, particularly where the ratio is concerned. The nature of the ratio is such that the company's labor costs decrease as bonuses increase, so that the company as well as the employees have a strong interest in improved bonuses. The Memorandum of Understanding states that accounting practices will show what adjustments, if any, are necessary to protect the equity of both parties in the benefits of the Plan. Thus the element of bargaining is left for other issues that traditionally have been considered bargainable. Both management and employees are able to spend their energies on better productivity instead of arguing over the standard.

The Scanlon Plan bonus is paid monthly in order to remunerate participants as closely as possible to the time when the bonus was earned. In a dynamic economy we have found that one of the biggest problems is that management learns of problems after it is too late to do anything about them. A good bonus check reinforces the activity that took place in the previous month, whereas a poor bonus unleashes efforts to find out what was wrong before the problem accumulates over a period of time. In this sense the measurement when calculated monthly is a good tool of control for both management and labor. The bonus is paid by separate check, so the worker has a clear indication of the significance of the plan and the performance to his individual earnings.

Bonus is paid on a percentage basis in order to recognize skills and potential contribution. This provides incentive for management people as well as for the worker in the shop. Not only is the incentive aspect of this important but the percentage payment is based on the potential contribution of the individual to the total bonus pool. The earnings of each individual are in the ratio; hence, potential savings under the ratio are proportionate to the individual earnings. The pressures of dissatisfaction over inequities arising out of the wage structure are aimed at the wage structure and not at the bonus system. This helps to protect the Plan from such inequities and maintains the integrity of collective bargaining by keeping such problems for collective bargaining rather than circumventing negotiations through the Plan.

The final but probably the most important principle which should be discussed is that the measurement is an integral part of a complete program for improving productivity. The measurement has not been used as the sole device to stimulate performance but only as a measure of improvement and a basis for maintaining the equity of the participating parties. The program for improvement involves the participation of all the experts in each department (namely, the people on the job) collaborating their ideas and their efforts toward the common objective.

When a company starts talking efficiency, its union's first thought is "speed up," because under narrow individual standards the only dimensions of production that typically confront the worker are the quantity and quality of a particular part going through his operation. Better efficiency can only mean more parts and better parts. The

Scanlon Plan opens up a broad area with an infinite number of dimensions, which the worker can influence through his production committee. When held up by scheduling or planning, the worker can quickly contribute his ideas on how the flow of work might better be organized. When the worker runs into faulty material or purchased parts, the production committee provides not only an avenue for communicating the problem to the purchasing agent but provides the assurance of a report that the supplier has been notified and corrective action is being taken. In this way the worker is able to influence many factors that govern his effectiveness on the job, factors which in the total picture are much more important than his speed on the job.

The Relationship of the Measurement to Communication and Cooperation

The Scanlon Plan ratio differs from other measurements in that it is part of a total program for increasing productivity. Other essays in this book deal specifically with the nature and functions of the production and screening committees. In this section, however, we will observe the use of the measurement in a hypothetical committee meeting to illustrate the principles that have been outlined in the preceding section.

In the monthly meetings of the screening committee the first topic on the agenda is to discuss the performance and the bonus for the previous month. This brings forth questions concerning external factors that influence performance. Orders have been declining, making it more difficult to maintain a steady flow of work through the plant. The vice president of sales outlines the problems that salesmen are running into out in the field. Some of these problems involve business conditions which we can't do much about, but others involve the cost, quality, and promptness of delivery of the products we are trying to sell. Sales warns us also that product mix is shifting against us, because we are not meeting competition in certain product lines, and indicates the areas of improvement necessary to get more business in these lines.

A worker asks why inventory went down when his department assembled more units than usual. The accountant breaks down the inventory figures to show that, while inventory increased in some areas, it declined in total because shipments were heavy and we did not shear as much material for process as usual due to the low volume of orders. Sales is admonished to keep the orders coming in.

The accountant is then asked to report on Sales Returns. He passes out a list of figures which have been mimeographed so that a copy can be taken back to each department. These figures show the products that were returned by customers during the month and the reasons why customers were dissatisfied. It is apparent that most of the returns involved a particular mechanism in a relatively new product. The employee representative from the machine shop asserts that they are still having trouble machining the parts that are causing the trouble and feels that this operation requires closer tolerances than our equipment can hold. The plant manager reports that the new piece of equipment which we ordered will arrive in two weeks and will help to solve the machining problems on this job. He asks the screening committeemen to pass the word along and get the production committee working on ideas that will facilitate getting the equipment set up and into production as fast as possible. The vice president of sales reminds us that there is a great potential market for this new product if we can keep our customers satisfied.

The committee then examines the payroll figures. The company president announces that the reason the Office and Salary Payroll is higher this month is that they have stepped up the work in research and development in order to get a new product into production as soon as possible. He describes the new product and the company's plans for pushing it in place of a product which had been steadily declining in sales. The added research personnel will make it somewhat harder to earn a bonus for the next few months, but our future bonuses and, more important, future employment depend on our ability to meet the growing competition in new products.

Having examined the past month's performance, the committee turns to the prospects for the future. The president indicates that orders have picked up recently, and, if we can meet our shipment schedule, bonus opportunity in the present month appears to be excellent. The accountant, however, is much less optimistic because he has been watching the daily shipment record and for the first ten days shipments were substantially behind the schedule. Everyone wants to know why shipments are lagging. The plant manager complains that finished units have been ready on schedule, but the shipping department has not been able to ship one very large order because there had been a mistake in ordering the containers, and when they arrived they were too small. The committeeman from the shearing department suggests that three or four men from his department could go down to shipping and help modify the containers so that we can get the shipment out this month, as work is slack in shearing because special materials that were ordered for a new job have been late in arriving. The plant manager agrees that this is a good idea and promises to have materials and tools available in the shipping room first thing in the morning. The personnel director reminds the committee that in cases of temporary transfer to meet emergencies like this, the workers involved receive the rate of the new job or carry their old wage rate, whichever is the higher.

The accountant is still pessimistic about the bonus opportunity, because even though we are able to crate and ship that order, inventory will still suffer due to the reduced materials going into process through the shearing department. The vice president of sales, who is very happy to see a problem solved to the satisfaction of one customer, is not pleased at all by the realization that lack of materials in shearing today means an unhappy customer tomorrow. But everyone agrees that it is better to have four men making crates for units that can be shipped than to have them waiting to shear material that has not arrived.

Then the committeeman from maintenance remembers that three years ago we had a similar job that required special stock. After the stock was sheared the order was canceled, and as there were no jobs on which the stock could be used, it was given to maintenance to store in the basement. The chief engineer does not think that the old stock will fit the dimensions of this particular job, but one of the committeemen who worked on that job three years ago is pretty sure that it can be used and reminds the committee that if it can be used it will not only save the Plan the labor cost of shearing new material, but also will save the company material costs on the job and will enable us to meet the delivery schedule. The president asks the plant manager to look at this material and put it into process if it can be used.

After the bonus figures have been screened, the bonus is announced over the loud speaker and the committee proceeds with the month's suggestions. After the screening meeting the plant manager calls all his foremen together and outlines the figures which the foremen will take up in their next production meeting. The machine-shop foreman is instructed to discuss the Sales Returns and elicit suggestions on how those parts may be improved. The shearing-department foreman and the foreman in the shipping room are told of the decision to transfer four men down to the shipping room to work on containers. Other suggestions which require further study and evaluation are discussed, and each foreman agrees to study the suggestions involving his department and to report to the plant manager within one week.

Conclusion

It will be noted from the foregoing screening meeting that the interest of all participants was directed toward many of the same figures which concern the board of directors of the company: sales, inventory, labor costs, orders, returns, and schedules. From an examination of these figures questions were asked relating to quality of product, delivery schedules, materials, new products—in short, the variables that determine the success of the enterprise. Without ever mentioning the speed of the individual worker, ideas and plans were presented in an effort to deal with the conditions and problems that were revealed in the figures.

Without such discussion and participation the measurement would be just another standard providing an "incentive" for speed-up. Without good leadership in using the measurement as a focal point for discussion and decision making, the committee meeting would be just another bull session without objectives, orientation, or guidance. Thus is can be seen that the Scanlon Plan ratio is an integral part of a program that is much broader than the typical incentive system, whether individual or group. Used properly, the ratio can be a tool to promote initiative, responsibility, and understanding on the part of all employees in the enterprise.

The specific ratio that has been developed in this essay is not the only type that has been used under the Scanlon Plan. In one application the measurement involved the relationship of labor costs to a physical measure of total production. In other cases variations of the Sales Value of Production concept have been designed to meet special needs or the limitations of the particular accounting system. It is this writer's belief, however, that the ratio discussed here provides the best medium to facilitate interest and understanding of the total enterprise. It has never been considered a perfectly accurate measure of productivity but derives its greatest strength from its simplicity and the sense of equity that develops from relating bonus earnings to the same variables that determine the success of the company.

7 . . . .

Problems under the Plan:

Summaries of

Conference Workshops

As in previous conferences, there were four workshop sessions at the 1957 Scanlon Plan Conference. Those attending the conference chose to participate in workshops by function or interest. Top-line managers attended the Management Workshop led by Professor Douglass V. Brown; union officers participated in the union session under the leadership of Herman Daigneault, President of the local Steelworkers' Union at Lapointe Machine Tool Company; controllers and accountants attended the Accounting Workshop with Elbridge S. Puckett of M.I.T. as moderator; and the personnel and industrial relations directors participated in the session led by Charles A. Myers.

In each of these sessions, there was give-and-take between the participants. Some had experience with the Scanlon Plan and reported on it; some had problems on which they needed help; and some were skeptical and asked questions before they would go further with the Plan. No transcription was taken, as discussions were "off the record," but the moderators of each workshop have summarized the main points below.

Summary: Management Session

DOUGLASS V. BROWN, *Moderator*

At the management session, most of the discussion stemmed from questions put by representatives of companies not operating under the Scanlon Plan and directed toward representatives of those companies operating under the Plan. To the observer, the most interesting aspect of the discussion was the obvious differences in the degrees of importance attached to particular problems by the respective groups.

The differences were particularly marked in those questions relating to the general area of management prerogatives. These were clearly matters of paramount importance to those companies without the Plan; to those companies having the Plan, the questions seemed insignificant, if not unintelligible. This is not to say that the companies with the Plan had relinquished their "prerogatives" or that they were not interested in managing, but rather that they were operating in an atmosphere where the classical questions of prerogatives had little or no meaning.

Along similar lines, companies without the Plan pressed many questions with respect to the timing and mechanism of changing the ratio. Companies with the Plan felt that there were very few occasions that would call for revising the ratio but that, if such an occasion arose, there would be no difficulty in arriving at an appropriate revision. There was the general feeling that, on these rare occasions, the ratio would be "arrived at" rather than "negotiated."

Other questions that bothered companies without the Plan had to do with such matters as setting standards, estimating costs, and maintaining performance from operators whose piecework earnings had been frozen at high levels. Companies with the Plan reported no important problems in these areas. Standards, in the sense of performance requirements, were outmoded by other aspects of the Plan. Costs, it was felt, could be better estimated from actual records than from engineering studies. Any decline in the direct output of employees formerly on piecework was more than offset by the effects resulting from their willingness to share the tricks of the trade with other employees.

There was general agreement that, under the Plan, jurisdictional problems had disappeared, that formal grievances had declined to insignificant numbers, and that absenteeism had been reduced. There was also general agreement that the quality of suggestions was, typically, on a high level. There was some feeling, however, that the volume and quality of suggestions showed a tendency to decline over time unless measures were taken periodically to rekindle the drive along these lines.

One problem mentioned by several of the companies operating under the Plan was that of "selling" top management on the idea of the Plan, particularly at the outset.

To try to summarize all too briefly: it seemed clear to this observer that companies without the Plan were deeply concerned with the "formulas," with the techniques of the Plan. To those companies with the Plan, the important thing was the atmosphere, and techniques played a relatively insignificant role in their thinking. The seemingly trite phrase "a way of life" was used over and over again; but the sincerity of expression and the collateral documentation robbed the phrase of its triteness.

Summary: Union Session
HERMAN DAIGNEAULT, *Moderator*

The primary subject for discussion with union officials at the conference was the manner in which current wage-incentive systems must be supplemented or amended for the benefit of those concerned and yet remain equitable to the operating of the Plan. Representatives from the various plants operating under the Plan described many of their experiences, which when summarized, show that there is no formula that can be adopted to meet this problem. Nevertheless, amicable settlements have been agreed upon and are operating satisfactorily. Various methods were used in the process.

Another question discussed was "How can increased productivity be achieved without a so-called speed-up?" Union representatives from companies with the Plan stated that there were many areas other than physical effort that can result in a substantial increase in productivity. Production suggestions, new methods, and cooperation among fellow workers have resulted in great increases in productivity in particular cases. Examples were given in which employees, free from the worries that are the scourge of an individual incentive plan and with no further concern about the type of work that they or anyone else were doing, turned out more pieces with less physical effort and much more peace of mind.

Inevitably, discussion turned to the question of an inborn fear that the company might take advantage of the productive knowledge that workers had obtained and take steps to maintain and possibly increase this level of productivity without any further regard to the Plan. At this time it was very strongly stated that this Plan definitely does not in any way terminate any of the rights that the union has and that this attitude has never been experienced in any Scanlon Plan installations. In all of these cases, both the unions and the companies have recognized and evaluated the benefits attained and have reached the conclusion that, through active participation and cooperation, they have strengthened their respective organizations, rather than weakened them.

A final question for consideration was, "What changes take place in labor-management relations?" Although the discussion brought out that unions have become somewhat more flexible toward management under this Plan, it also emphasized that this flexibility in no way infringed on any rights to which members were entitled under their respective collective-bargaining agreements. Even though the unions hold strong to their principles, they do not lose sight of the fact that by sincere cooperation, which often means "talking it out," solutions are found to problems not covered by the collective agreement.

Summary: Accounting Session
E. S. Puckett, *Moderator*

The opening discussion concentrated largely on the details of computing and paying the bonus, so that the newcomers to the Plan would have a firm foundation for exploring more involved aspects of the ratio. As to the payment of Scanlon Plan bonus it was generally agreed that paying bonus as a percentage of gross earnings satisfied the requirements of federal wage and hour legislation. Those companies that have consulted wage and hour administrators have found that a production bonus paid monthly must be paid on overtime premium.

With respect to the year-end reserve, it is an almost universal practice to divide the reserve pool by the total monthly bonuses that have been paid during the year. Each participant is then paid the resulting percentage payout on the basis of his total bonus checks. From an accounting standpoint this is the easiest way to compute and pay the reserve, and it insures that each individual will receive his equity in the reserve in terms of his total earnings during months in which a bonus was earned.

Several of the new companies expressed an interest in product mix and fluctuations in the ratio resulting from shifts in product mix. Three firms which had several years of experience with the Plan described situations in which the labor content in one product line may be as much as twice the labor content in other products. Two of these companies live quite successfully with a single ratio and have found that monthly fluctuations in bonus opportunity do not create misapprehension and disturbances with employees, *if* they clearly understand the economic forces involved. In fact, these companies have found that a single ratio has had tremendous educational value in terms of focusing attention on problems with which management has always had to contend. The third company applied separate ratios on the two major product lines and found that this approach also met with success.

A discussion of the various questions concerning the application of the Plan to multidivisional operations generated considerable interest, particularly from the larger firms. One firm in the initial stages of exploring the Plan wondered if it could be applied separately to three divisions operating under one roof and comprising one bargaining unit. The experience of several firms with similar circumstances indicated that it is most desirable to install the Plan in the largest possible unit. One firm had applied a single measurement for two plants located sixty miles apart and found that the resulting communication among the management and employees of the two plants more than offset the difficulties of traveling sixty miles each month for screening meetings. Another firm applied a single measurement to three large divisions operating at the same location. In this case it was found that, although separate screening committees functioned in each division, it was much healthier to have everyone earning bonus on the total performance rather than on a divisional basis—particularly where a single local union represented all production employees. The experience of another company suggested that much thought must be given to the ultimate goal envisaged for the Plan. If it is intended that the entire plant may at some point be included in the Plan, it should be recognized that it is extremely difficult to start with one group and later attempt to add additional groups. The experience in this situation indicated that once the initial group has achieved a measure of success under the Plan, the people are afraid of doing anything that might "rock the boat."

Another problem involving multidivisional operations occurred in a plant where the office workers spend one-third of their time working for a division not included in the Plan. It was felt that the office workers should participate in the Plan and that they should not be penalized because some of their work fell outside the division. Accordingly, only two-thirds of the office payroll was included in the development of the ratio and in the monthly computation of the bonus percentage, but each month the company contributes additional funds to provide full participation for the office workers.

Following the discussion of questions raised by the new companies, interest turned to the current problems of firms with some experience under the Plan. A question asked by several was whether there was any experience to indicate the desirability of having a specified management person to be responsible for following up suggestions and their disposition and for keeping communication lines intact. Only one firm (one involving 7000 employees) has delegated these responsibilities to one person. Others have felt that the management person in each department should be responsible for suggestions related to that area and have made it the responsibility of the personnel manager to receive the suggestions from the production committees and to prepare the agenda for the screening committee.

One of the most significant conclusions, at least from the accountants' standpoint, concerned the accounting function in relation to overall company operation. Many accountants found that after the Plan went into effect in their companies they were able to make a much bigger contribution to the total operation than ever before. The first responsibility that the accountant has had to assume is that of explaining to the screening committee the figures which make up the monthly bonus calculation. The inventory variation is one factor that is particularly difficult to understand, and the accountants have made particular efforts to explain this aspect of the computation in clear and understandable terms. A second, and equally important, responsibility is to keep the committees and departments informed with respect to production, costs, and any areas that need special efforts toward improvement. Thus, the accountant is not only making a direct contribution to the work force in terms of understanding the bonus computation but also finds that he is raised from the area of straight bookkeeping and is helping people to utilize accounting data to effect concrete results.

It was also brought out in the discussion that management must also bring to the meetings relevant information concerning sales, customer returns, complaints, production bottlenecks, or any concrete problems which must be faced and dealt with by the cooperative efforts of all employees. Future plans concerning the introduction of new equipment and new processes are important areas where worker receptivity is greatly enhanced by communication of such plans and solicitation of related suggestions.

Summary: Personnel Session
Charles A. Myers, *Moderator*

The workshop session with personnel or industrial-relations directors started with a discussion of how the personnel director's job is affected by the Scanlon Plan. This brought out quite clearly that fewer grievances come to the personnel department for consideration, since the Plan tends to focus employee and union attention on production problems, and grievances are solved more informally or are not raised at all. Further points made were that the Plan eliminates conflicts between direct and indirect workers and that it helps labor understand the need for technological change—another thorny personnel problem in the past.

Participants from companies with the Plan, however, stressed that the personnel director now has additional duties under the Plan. He is forced to take the leadership in explaining management's actions more clearly. In some cases he helps administer the Plan, serving as secretary in the top screening committee and otherwise assisting members of the committee in performing their duties.

After this initial discussion, the conferees turned to some of the questions that were raised by some of the companies that were contemplating the introduction of the Plan. One particularly lively discussion was generated by these questions: "If you start this plan, aren't you legally obligated to bargain on many other things?" "Shouldn't management's obligations be spelled out in writing, so that a sharp line is drawn between what management agrees to do and what it reserves for itself?" The reply from the companies with the Plan was that this was never a problem. Both management and labor "grow up" and attain greater maturity. Workers understand the need of the company to make a profit, and management understands labor's desire for more and more information about costs, prices, competitive bids, and so forth. In some companies the formal Memorandum of Understanding has never even been signed, and no one has challenged management prerogatives. All of those with the Plan agreed that management was forced to do a better job, that the Plan kept management on its toes, but none thought that management had been damaged in this process.

Some of the representatives from companies considering adoption of the Plan wanted to know whether the Plan strengthened the local union. Discussion brought out that union members are more vitally interested in what goes on under the Plan, and rotating membership on the committees gives wider participation in this union-management activity. Time spent on grievance handling is reduced, and discussions of production suggestions are increased. There was also some discussion on the attitude of the national union toward this Plan. Variations were pointed out between unions, but most of those companies with the Plan had no difficulties.

Communication problems under the Plan were also discussed. The Stromberg-Carlson representatives indicated how the public-address system had been used to explain the screening-committee results and bonus achievements. Other companies used employee observers in screening committees to pass on information. One company called the foremen together immediately after the screening-committee action so that management's channel of communication could be as rapid as the union's. All agreed that foremen, as members of management, were placed in positions of real leadership as a consequence of the Plan. They found that they had to plan the work, get materials, assign jobs so as to make production go more smoothly, and no longer had to drive men to do their jobs, since the Plan unleashed creative energies in themselves. Thus, while the foremen were forced to do a better job, it was of a different dimension, and one that made their task easier and more pleasant in many ways. There was not the same friction as there was before the Plan was adopted.

PART THREE.......

Evaluation

DOUGLAS MCGREGOR

8 . . . .

The Scanlon Plan through a Psychologist's Eyes

The Scanlon Plan is a philosophy of organization. It is not a program in the usual sense; it is a way of life—for the management, for the union, and for every individual employee. Because it is a way of life, it affects virtually every aspect of the operation of the organization. In this fact lies its real significance.

Underlying Joseph Scanlon's efforts was a deep and fundamental belief in the worth of the human individual, in his capacity for growth and learning, in his ability to contribute significantly "with his head as well as his hands" to the success of the company which employs him. Scanlon, unlike many who make similar professions, really respected human beings.

The Scanlon Plan is what he evolved out of his experience to implement his fundamental belief in people. Although he was anything but a theoretician and although he was only casually familiar with the research findings of the social sciences, the Plan he conceived fulfills to a remarkable degree the requirements for effective organized human effort that have been highlighted by such research. In addition, the actual experiences of Scanlon Plan companies provide significant verification of the predictions the social scientist makes on theoretical grounds.

The Plan implements Scanlon's underlying belief by establishing three broad conditions within which it becomes possible and natural for all members of the firm to collaborate in contributing to its economic effectiveness. These conditions are:

1. A formally established "area of collaboration" and machinery (production and screening committees) for coordinating such collaborative efforts throughout the whole organization. This is accomplished without undermining collective bargaining or weakening the local union.

2. A meaningful, realistic, common objective (the "ratio") in terms of which such collaborative efforts can be objectively measured.

3. A psychologically adequate system of rewards (noneconomic as well as economic) for a wide range of contributions to the effectiveness of the enterprise. (Traditional incentive wages, profit sharing, and suggestions system awards are quite inadequate in terms of modern psychological theory.)

As a consequence of establishing these three conditions, the employees and the managements of Scanlon Plan companies literally discover a new way of life. The process is not easy; some of the learning is rough indeed. There is little of a sentimental sweetness-and-light atmosphere, but there develops a mutual respect which cuts across even the most violent disagreements. The new relationship permeates in surprising but meaningful ways into every corner of the organization. It is some of these consequences and their relation to social-science theory and findings that I would like to examine.

Scientific Management and Human Capabilities

Many research studies have pointed out that, however persuasive the *logic* of "scientific management" may be, the consequences of its application are often contrary to expectation.[1] Informal but effective collusion to defeat managerial purposes takes many forms, and it is widespread. Less recognized, but perhaps more important than these consequences, is the failure of this approach to make effective use of the potentialities of people. Treating the worker as though he were,

[1] Chris Argyris, *Personality and Organization*, New York: Harper, 1957. Chapters IV and V summarize the data succinctly.

in Drucker's words, a "glorified machine tool" [2] is a shameful waste of the very characteristics which distinguish people from machines.

Despite protests to the contrary, the approach of scientific management has been to treat the worker as a "hand" rather than a human being. The consequences of so doing have been attributed to the "natural" cussedness of workers and explained as the price of technological efficiency. Pleasant working surroundings and fringe benefits have been used to alleviate the negative aspects of assembly-line jobs. Fancy communications programs and Madison Avenue sales gimmicks have been used to persuade the worker of the vital importance of his tiny contribution to the enterprise. These are understandable but largely ineffective palliatives. However, work simplification and all the other paraphernalia of the industrial engineer —consistent with a view of the worker as a glorified machine tool— remain the commonly accepted way to utilize human effort in industry.

Scanlon knew better. He knew that what Drucker calls "industrial citizenship" [3] is perfectly possible even in the mass-production setting, provided management will recognize that workers have brains and ingenuity as well as muscles. The Scanlon Plan creates the necessary conditions for this discovery. Once these conditions are established, people collaborate because it is to their interest to do so. They don't need to be made to "feel" important; they *are* important and they know it.

The most far-reaching consequence of this creation of genuine industrial citizenship is the virtual elimination of what Argyris calls the sense of "psychological failure" created by the traditional approach of scientific management. Among other things, the notion of the "nonproductive" worker, and the "burden" concept of staff and administrative employees go out the window. Productivity, under the Scanlon Plan, is not confined to direct production workers, nor is the line organization the only part of the enterprise that is seen as carrying its own weight. Productivity is measured by reduction of the labor bill, and *everyone* can contribute to this objective.

Improvement of the ratio, by every means, is everybody's business. The individual's contribution is not limited to doing "a fair day's work." The janitor and the stenographer, as well as the engineer and the manager, can, and often do, exercise human ingenuity in develop-

---

[2] Peter Drucker, *The Practice of Management*, New York: Harper, 1954, pp. 280 ff.

[3] Peter Drucker, *The New Society*, New York: Harper, 1949, pp. 151 ff.

ing improvements entirely outside the limits of their own job descriptions. The area for collaboration covers anything that will contribute to the effectiveness of the enterprise.

The challenging opportunities that are inherent in every industrial organization for people to assume responsibility, achieve status, acquire new skills, learn, develop, exercise creativity become apparent once this area of collaboration is carved out. The idea that workers are paid to do what they are told and management is paid to tell them not only prevents effective collaboration but automatically creates the feeling of psychological failure. It leads either to indifferent passivity or to active hostility. Genuine participation in problem solving removes the causes of these common reactions.

The Task of Management

It should not be supposed that management loses its responsibility to manage under a Scanlon Plan. Much to the contrary. One of the happier consequences is that the foreman ceases to occupy the impossible role that has been his in recent years and becomes a manager in the real sense of the term. He is no longer caught in the problem of divided loyalties and conflicting pressures. He is no longer the pawn of a variety of staff groups who "control" him to death under the label of serving him. He ceases to be a paper shuffler, an ineffective disciplinarian, a "master and victim of doubletalk," [4] and becomes a manager willy-nilly. Sometimes the pressures that bring about this transformation are painful in the extreme. However, most supervisors come to relish their new role.

Further up the line there is considerably less tilting with the windmill of prerogatives and more genuine concern with managing the enterprise. One of the interesting phenomena among management people in Scanlon Plan companies is their inability to comprehend the questions that are frequently asked of them concerning their freedom to manage. Authority in the sense of the right to be arbitrary, to force subordinates to do their bidding, ceases to be a meaningful idea because the collaborative relationship almost eliminates the necessity for this kind of order giving.

The management task in Scanlon-Plan companies becomes one of genuine leadership. The manager who is primarily a power seeker and a protector of management's right to be arbitrary finds little satisfaction in such a situation. The pattern of managerial behavior

---

[4] Fritz Roethlisberger, "The Foreman: Master and Victim of Doubletalk," *Harvard Business Review*, Vol. 23, No. 3, Spring, 1945, pp. 283-298.

which tends to emerge is remarkably close to that of the "democratic" leader in the classic Lewin and Lippitt research.[5] However, this term "democratic" does not mean abdication; it does not imply that "everyone decides everything." Its essence is that it makes effective use of human resources through participation; it provides general rather than close supervision; it is "employee-centered"[6] it encourages responsible behavior and tough-minded self-control rather than reliance on external authority.

As mentioned above, disagreements flourish in Scanlon Plan companies. Management has the responsibility and exercises the authority in their resolution. The difference is that people usually disagree about the best way to do the job or to reduce costs or to improve the profit margin rather than about whose rights are what or what legalistic interpretation should be put on a work rule. This is a big difference.

The Scanlon Plan typifies Drucker's "management by objectives and self-control." General (as opposed to close) supervision and wide delegation evolve naturally as management discovers that it is no longer necessary to force people to do what needs to be done. It becomes possible to deal with people as mature adults rather than as children and thus to avoid much of the conflict between organizational requirements and the needs of the human personality which Argyris has so well delineated.[7]

Cooperation and Competition

The psychological significance of all of this is that the Scanlon Plan "fits together" the purposes of organization with the natural human tendency to collaborate when collaboration is the sensible way to do things. Industrial organizations are complex *interdependent* human entities. Unless the many related functions are smoothly interlocked, unless people are constantly adjusting to each other in terms of common objectives, organizations cannot operate effectively.

Emphasis on individual competition, on narrow job responsibilities, and antagonism toward the natural tendency of humans to form groups characterize much of present-day managerial practice. This emphasis is 180 degrees out of phase with the need for collaboration in a complex system of interdependence.

[5] Kurt Lewin, Ronald Lippitt, and Ralph K. White, "Patterns of Aggressive Behavior in Experimentally Created Social Climates," *Journal of Social Psychology*, Vol. X, 1939, pp. 271–299.

[6] Rensis Likert, "Motivational Dimensions of Administration," *America's Manpower Crisis*, Chicago: Public Administration Service, 1956.

[7] Chris Argyris, *op. cit.*

The Scanlon Plan sets a meaningful common objective and creates the necessary conditions to bring practice and organizational need into phase. Instead of lip service to "teamwork" within a system which stacks the cards against it, the Scanlon Plan makes teamwork the natural way of life. And then it becomes no longer necessary to preach about its value!

Competitive motivations—also natural to humans—are not ignored either. However, instead of competing with fellow workers, or saying, "To hell with the other department (or the other shift); I'm paid to do my job, not to worry about them," the competition is with other companies in the industry. In a capitalist economy what could be more natural?

Resistance to Change

A fair amount of research has pointed up the fact that resistance to change is a reaction primarily to certain methods of instituting change rather than an inherent human characteristic.[8] Leo Moore and Herbert Goodwin of the M.I.T. School of Industrial Management have coined the term "improvement management" to describe a way of gaining some of the benefits of scientific management without producing resistance to change.[9] The Scanlon Plan minimizes such resistance because it involves people in the process of creating change rather than imposing it on them. Improvement management is the Scanlon way of life because everyone is interested in improving the ratio.

Significant examples of worker-generated change in the organization of work are common in Scanlon Plan companies. Ironically, these are frequently changes that management tried unsuccessfully to introduce in pre-Scanlon days. Resistance becomes instead active instigation. In fact, the Scanlon Plan company experience with the change process is one of the most clear-cut examples of the way in which the research-based predictions of social science are fulfilled in practice.[10]

[8] Alvin Zander, "Resistance to Change: Its Analysis and Prevention," *Advanced Management*, Vol. 15, No. 1, January, 1950, pp. 9–11.

[9] Leo Moore, "Too Much Management, Too Little Change," *Harvard Business Review*, Vol. 34, No. 1, January–February, 1956, pp. 41–48.

[10] See, for example: Lester Coch and John R. P. French, Jr., "Overcoming Resistance to Change," *Human Relations*, Vol. I, 1948, pp. 512–532; Kurt Lewin, "Group Decision and Social Change," *Readings in Social Psychology*, rev. ed., New York: Henry Holt, 1952, pp. 459–473; A. T. M. Wilson, "Some Contrasting Cocio-Technical Production Systems," *The Manager*, December, 1955.

It is perhaps needless to point out that restriction of output, feather-bedding, collusion to fudge production records, and all the other ingenious group methods of defeating the managerial purposes of traditional incentive plans disappear completely in Scanlon Plan companies. Again, this is exactly what the social scientist would predict on the basis of his research into the causes of these phenomena.[11]

Human Motivation

Examination of modern theories of motivation points up further Scanlon's insight into human behavior. The Scanlon Plan production and screening committees, as well as the whole management-employee relationship which develops, provide ideal means for satisfying ego and self-actualization needs which are typically frustrated under the conditions of present-day industrial employment.[12]

There is no undervaluation of economic motives either. However, one happy consequence of the Scanlon Plan is the minimization of conflict over the workers' share of the proceeds of enterprise. The ratio is determined from accounting data, and even in unionized companies there is no instance on record of an impasse over this issue! [13]

The economic rewards of the Scanlon Plan are fully consistent with present-day psychological knowledge. First, they are related to factors in the work situation which are controllable by employees. This is in contrast to most profit-sharing plans. Under the latter workers are rewarded in a fashion which is only remotely connected to their direct contribution. (I know of one profit-sharing plan where the profits which were shared for several years resulted primarily from the speculation of the treasurer of the company in the raw-materials market!)

Second, the payoff is within a sensible time span. It is well established that rewards become less effective the more remote in time

---

[11] William Foote Whyte, *Money and Motivation*, New York: Harper, 1955.

[12] Abraham Maslow, *Motivation and Personality*, New York: Harper, 1954, especially Chapters 4, 5, 8; Douglas McGregor, "The Human Side of Enterprise," *Management Review*, November, 1957, pp. 22–28; E. Wight Bakke, *The Unemployed Worker*, New Haven: Yale University Press, 1940; Robert W. White, *Lives in Progress*, New York: Dryden Press, 1952.

[13] Scanlon was insistent—and wisely so—that the Plan offer management no escape from meeting the standards of wage levels and other conditions of employment established generally by collective bargaining. To use it in this fashion would be the surest way to undermine the union's acceptance of the philosophy of collaboration. The Scanlon Plan would quickly be seen as a device to negate the legitimate gains of the labor movement.

they are from the behavior which is being rewarded. An annual pay-off (typical under profit sharing) is too remote to be of much use as a motivator. The monthly payoff under the Scanlon Plan is mean-ingfully related in time to the behavior which affects the ratio.

Third, the plant-wide nature of the bonus is realistic in terms of the common objectives of the members of the enterprise. It does not eliminate individual differences in wage rates related to job responsi-bilities, but it creates the proper perception of "sharing" in a common endeavor.

Fourth, the bonus is paid for *all* contributions to the effectiveness of the enterprise rather than for the narrow contribution of output per man-hour which is common under conventional incentive plans. There are no problems in relating pay to fancy (and largely unreal-istic) "standards" for measuring individual performance, particularly for maintenance, clerical, and other service jobs. Moreover, there is no longer any incentive to defeat the time-study engineer or to hide jigs and fixtures which have been invented to "beat the standard" or to establish collusive relations with tool-crib clerks, timekeepers, inspectors, and others in order to "make out." [14]

Finally, the payoff reflects the success of the enterprise in under-standable terms. There is no necessity for interpreting the elaborate formulas of the industrial engineers (which workers are quite able to do, by the way), or for fathoming the formalized and often mis-leading gobbledygook of the balance sheet.

Mention of the balance sheet leads to one other economic point I would emphasize: the education for all participants in the economics of enterprise. American management has spent many millions of dollars in attempts to provide economic education to workers. The results have not been measured, but one may be permitted a certain skepticism.[15]

The Scanlon Plan, however, provides such education in the most direct fashion: through day-by-day involvement in the problems of the enterprise. A casual conversation with Scanlon Plan company employees often reveals an understanding of our economic system which is uncommon even among college graduates. And this funda-mental and important educative process costs not one cent! It re-quires no films or brochures or discussion groups or lecturers. It is obtained in the normal course of daily life by direct, firsthand experi-

[14] William Foote Whyte, *op. cit.*, particularly Chapter 7.

[15] William H. Whyte, *Is Anybody Listening*, New York: Simon & Schuster, 1952; Douglas Williams in *Management Education for Itself and Its Employees*, New York: A.M.A., 1954, Part 4.

ence. Scanlon Plan company employees are believers in capitalism, and they know *why* they are!

Staff-Line Conflict

Friction between workers and lower levels of supervision on the one hand and staff departments such as industrial engineering, accounting, personnel, inspection, inventory control, purchasing, and research and development on the other hand is widespread in industry today, and it is a good deal more costly than management usually recognizes. Research studies and reports of participant observers have provided substantial evidence of these phenomena.[16]

A major cause of these frictions is the fact that staff departments are placed in the position of imposing their standards, their plans and procedures, their "expertness" on the line. This is a fact quite generally despite textbook assertions that the staff functions are those of service, advice, and counsel. The staff engineer tells the worker to "follow the blueprint" even when (as happens all too often) the worker's knowledge of his tools and materials tells him that this is foolish or impossible. A substantial amount of paper work by the supervisor is summarized or scrutinized by the accounting department and turned over to others higher in the organization to be used frequently in a disciplinary manner ("Your variances are out of line," or "You have overrun your budget," or "You made an unauthorized expenditure").

The simple psychological fact is that external controls of this kind engender hostility and lead to the exercise of a substantial degree of ingenuity directed solely toward defeating the purposes of those who have instigated the controls. This is the exact opposite of management's desire; it is the antithesis of collaboration. Unfortunately, management at the top is rarely aware of the extensiveness of this internecine warfare, and the staff groups tend to interpret it as evidence of the stupidity or inherent hostility of workers and supervisors. The typical staff reaction is to tighten and elaborate the controls, which of course simply makes matters worse.[17]

[16] William Foote Whyte, *op. cit.;* Chris Argyris, "Human Problems with Budgets," *Harvard Business Review*, Vol. 31, No. 1, January–February, 1953, pp. 97–110; Charles A. Myers and John G. Turnbull, "Line and Staff in Industrial Relations," *Harvard Business Review*, Vol. 34, No. 4, July–August, 1956, pp. 113–124; and F. J. Roethlisberger and William J. Dickson, *Management and the Worker*, Cambridge, Mass.: University Press, 1939, Part IV.

[17] See Argyris, "Human Problems with Budgets," *op. cit.*, for a penetrating analysis of this set of problems.

The Scanlon Plan, when these groups are included, creates entirely different relations between staff and line. The need for external controls diminishes to the vanishing point as collaboration toward the common objective of improving the ratio becomes the way of life. The staff groups can help the line in a great many ways if this is what they are set up to do. The line learns to use and to value this help as soon as the staff is relieved of a function which makes them appear to be policemen and spies. Evidence for this fundamental change in relations is to be found readily in Scanlon Plan companies. One nice example was the occasion at the Lapointe Machine Tool Company when the engineers voluntarily postponed their vacations in order to prepare specifications for a new order so that there would be sufficient work to avoid a layoff in the factory.[18]

If the Scanlon Plan accomplished nothing else but to bring about effective collaboration between staff and line it would be a major contribution to organizational effectiveness. But this consequence is simply one of a large number of by-products resulting from a changed way of life. It is, in addition, a convincing demonstration of the well-established psychological fact that self-control is far more effective than externally imposed authority.

Conclusion

There are other ramifications of the operation of the Scanlon Plan which fit consistently with the implications of modern social-science findings. However, those discussed above serve to document my initial assertion concerning this consistency. They demonstrate, also, the difference between the usual personnel "program" and a genuine organizational philosophy, an industrial way of life.

No doubt other patterns of relationship will be found which yield results comparable with or superior to the Scanlon Plan. It is probable that the Plan as Scanlon conceived it would be difficult to establish in some kinds of industrial situations even if both management and union desired it. However, I will venture the prediction that we will succeed in increasing our utilization of the human potential in organizational settings only as we succeed in creating conditions which generate a meaningful way of life.

Scanlon's lasting contribution is his recognition—now effectively

---

[18] Fred Lesieur tells how the machinists in this same company, during pre-Scanlon days, would receive with glee a set of engineering specifications containing a major error and build the equipment exactly "according to specs" with full knowledge that it would ultimately have to be scrapped!

demonstrated in action—that one cannot successfully tackle this central task of management with gimmicks or procedures or programs. The real task of management is to create conditions which result in genuine collaboration throughout the organization. To create such conditions is to establish a way of life. This is the central conclusion to which the findings of social science are pointing today. And this is the lesson that Joseph Scanlon taught us all.

9 . . . .

Variations in Environment

and the Scanlon Plan

How broadly applicable are the concepts underlying the Scanlon Plan? Spectacular success has been achieved in applying these concepts to a number of specific situations and this fact is widely recognized. But the transferability of this experience is, if anything, even more widely questioned. Joseph Scanlon was acutely aware of the questions and often discussed this point. I can hear him now, referring to his experiences in the Thirties with firms that were saved after verging on bankruptcy, "The experts would come and see for themselves and say, 'Joe, this is wonderful. It's a miracle. Things are happening here that I didn't think were possible. *BUT*, but, Joe, it wouldn't work if the firm hadn't been ready for the cleaners.'"

As Douglas McGregor has suggested, Joe enjoyed confounding the experts. Each of his situations was a little like Kettering's diesel locomotive: it wouldn't work, but there goes one down the tracks. And, as the Scanlon Plan developed, Joe, and Fred Lesieur along with him, have accumulated a great many "but stories": but it wouldn't work if the firm hadn't been profitable to begin with, in a multiplant company, where the workers are skilled, where they are unskilled, where the work force includes a lot of women, with any union other than the Steelworkers', and so on. The temptation is apparently strong for observers of the Plan's operation in any single case to attribute success there to the environmental conditions of that case and then to conclude that these special circumstances are at least necessary, if not sufficient, conditions for success elsewhere.

One of the most interesting and significant aspects of the conference reported here is the diversity of experience and of environmental conditions represented among the attending companies using the plan currently. Much of the discussion at the conference amounted really to an examination of this diversity, along with the problems that have surely accompanied installation and use of the Scanlon Plan under varying conditions. I will report on that discussion here, summarizing the environmental diversity represented and the view the parties have taken of problems resulting from their environments.

Environmental Diversity Represented at the Conference

Nineteen companies, twenty-one plants, and eighteen local unions using the Scanlon Plan were represented at the 1957 Conference. The environmental conditions encountered by these units can be reviewed under the following headings: size and structure of operations, economic conditions, job conditions, and labor relations.

Size and Structure

A frequent contention is that the Plan will work only in rather small plants, where the group is cohesive and communication problems are minimal. The range of sizes in plant units represented at the conference is thus of considerable interest. The tabulation shows that this range is far broader than is commonly assumed.

Number of Employees in Plants Using the Scanlon Plan and
Represented at the Conference

Number of Employees	Number of Plants
under 60	3
61–100	2
101–200	5
201–500	3
501–1000	5
1001–1500	2
over 1500 (7200)	1

The 1954 Census of Manufactures shows that about two-thirds of all manufacturing employees worked in establishments with average employment of 1000 or fewer employees and about one-fourth in establishments of 100 or less. Thus, the Plan operates in a range of plant sizes that includes most manufacturing employees.

In addition to this variety in plant size, there were a number of structural differences among the firms represented. In three cases, a firm operates more than one plant using the Scanlon Plan, with the products of the two plants being broadly similar. Of the nineteen firms included in the tabulation, nine are multiplant enterprises. In about half the cases, the financial structure of the firm is such that one individual or family group exercises policy control of operations. The size of the communities in which these plants are located also varies considerably, from small towns where the plant is a dominant or at least a very important factor in the local economy to larger and more metropolitan areas. In one case (the plant was not represented at the conference) the firm uses the Scanlon Plan in an English plant as well as one in the United States.

Economic Conditions

To diversity of size of plant, structure of the firm, and community environment must be added wide variation in the economic conditions faced by the Scanlon Plan groups, both at the time of the Plan's inception and over the period of time the Plan has been in use. If the firms are compared according to profitability with their own industries and at the time the Plan was started, this picture emerges:

Variations according to Profitability

Profitability Prior to Plan's Inception	Number of Firms
Losing money; close to liquidation	4
Below industry average but no immediate threat of closing	3
About average in the industry	9
Clearly better than industry average	3

This tabulation reflects the fact that the Plan has a special appeal in situations of economic adversity, partly because these are circumstances when labor and management can identify most clearly a common interest of immediate importance. But the tabulation also shows that threatened economic disaster is by no means a necessary condition for a successful Scanlon Plan.

All nineteen firms have made improvements in their profit positions since the Plan started, and all but one firm has, on the average, expanded its number of employees. Nevertheless, all nineteen firms have had ups and downs to contend with in employment, bonuses paid, and profits, and in a few cases the fluctuations have been extreme. Partly these fluctuations have reflected conditions in the economy generally and partly conditions in a given industry or segment of the industry. Discussion at the conference indicated that the Plan's value to the parties involved was apparently greatest during times of changing environmental conditions. These were often times of acute problems, which the parties felt were more readily identified, understood, and solved under Scanlon Plan conditions.

There were other important variations in the economic environments facing these organizations. The industries involved, all within the manufacturing sector of the economy, range from consumer goods, such as shoes, silverware, pens and pencils, to intermediate goods for use by other firms, such as door handles, clocks and other accessories for automobiles, industrial saws, concrete pipe, lockers, shelves, and products for the armed services, to capital goods, such as preserved railroad ties, tanks for processing chemicals, broaching machines, and packaging equipment.

These industries vary greatly in the intensity and nature of competition in the product market. Some of the firms operate under conditions where competition is intense; in other cases, the firm is the dominant producer of a certain product, or styling and sales effort play a dominant market role. The seasonal fluctuations in demand for these products vary widely. So does the proportion of total costs that appears in the firm's payrolls, as shown in the summary below:

Proportionate Importance of Labor Cost

Payrolls as a Proportion of Total Cost (per cent)	Number of Plants
15–25	3
26–35	9
36–45	7
46–55	2

It may be noted that the list of industries does not include a plant in the chemical, oil, or other processing group, where the labor cost is a very small proportion of total cost. The opportunities for problem-solving through union-management cooperation are certainly great in these industries, particularly in the areas of saving materials and reducing down time. Special care would doubtless have to be taken in such cases with the measurement and sharing of gains.

Job Conditions

The types of diversity already set forth suggest diversity in conditions on the job. That is indeed the case. The composition of the labor force varies from plants where the dominant group is female to plants where not a single woman graces the premises. In some cases, the work is almost exclusively unskilled and laborious, and in others professional, technical, and skilled manpower is quantitatively as well as qualitatively of great significance in the enterprise. There are plants producing long runs of fairly well-standardized items which make use of assembly-line methods of manufacture, and there are others which rarely produce two identical items, so that the conditions of the job-shop predominate.

The physical surroundings on the job vary widely from one plant to another. At least two of the plants are clearly showpieces of American industry: handsome on the outside as well as in, equipped with the most up-to-date machinery, air-conditioned, and so on. About some of the others, it can be said that they are safer and more pleasant places to work than they were when the Plan started, but they still leave much to be desired. In still other cases, the work is just inherently dirty and heavy and rough.

Labor Relations

Of the twenty-one plants under discussion here, all but three are unionized. In three cases, the union is independent; in fourteen plants, the union involved is affiliated with the A.F.L.–C.I.O., and the local union in the remaining plant is affiliated with District 50 of the United Mine Workers. Among the A.F.L.–C.I.O. affiliates, the United Steelworkers' and the International Association of Machinists predominate. In two plants, there are two local unions involved, one representing the skilled group, tool and die makers, and the other representing the production workers. In two other cases, office workers are organized and belong to the same local union as do the production workers.

By and large, the union-management relationship at the time the Plan started was amicable, as it is in a great many plants throughout the country. In three or possibly four cases, however, the relationship was rough if not bitter, with a strike preceding fairly closely the inception of the Plan. In general, the stronger and more intelligently militant the local, the more immediately successful has been the installation of the Plan, except in one case of a new local which was rather distrustful of management. In this last case, when the union more than the management was responsible for bringing in the Plan, the parties have had real difficulty learning how to work together. In a sense, they have tried "to run before they have walked" and, in the process, have stumbled a number of times.

The labor relationships, then, have been diverse, but generally orderly. The parties have had at least some respect for and understanding of each other, and personal relationships were, if not always cordial, at least not overly strained. Strength and militance on the part of the local have made for the success in the Plan; bitterness and distrust present serious difficulties.

The Parties' View of Problems Posed by the Environment

Our review of the environmental conditions faced by firms using the Scanlon Plan shows that the Plan can operate in a very great variety of situations. That is not the same as saying, however, that it can operate in any environment or that some conditions do not make for more difficulties than others. Discussion at the conference brought out that tough problems have been generated by the environment for all the plants represented and that some of these problems have been most difficult to resolve. But, as one of the conferees pointed out, the problems are there in any case. The Plan is not like a magic wand that makes them disappear. What it can provide is a way and a will to work with these problems. The real question is, then, are you better able to resolve them with the Plan than without it?

This question raises another that is critically involved in any assessment of the impact of the environment on use of the Scanlon Plan. What do you mean by "success"? This is a most difficult question to answer, for we are dealing with a set of principles and a general approach to solving the problems of the workplace. Success must be judged, then, more by the workability and productiveness of a process than by an ideal conception of how any given situation ought to look after the Plan's application.

For example, take the problems posed by the size of the unit. Just because the Plan operates in units of widely varying size, it doesn't follow that size has no effect. It would be silly to suppose that the intimate personal relationships and knowledge of the whole operation possible for everyone in a 40-man plant are possible in a plant employing 7200, or even a few hundred. Discussion at the conference brought out the greater complexity of committee structure needed in a larger plant, as well as the increased attention that must be paid to training new employees, giving them "the word" about the Plan and, in general, the constant problem of keeping people informed throughout the organization of what is going on and why. But size means increased complexity of organization and difficulty in communication in any case. The experience of the larger firms seemed to be that size was a problem, to be sure, but not one that made the Plan unworkable. On the contrary, the Plan helped both union and management do a better job of maintaining liaison and coherence in their organizations. At the same time, the problems encountered in the largest establishments using the Plan do suggest the advisability of keeping units as small as is consistent with other characteristics of the organization. Thus, in a large multiplant firm, it would probably be best not to cover the whole firm in one Plan, but to cover plants individually.

Another set of problems arises, however, in the case of a multiplant company. For example, in a large and sprawling enterprise the needs of small branch plants may not get much home-office attention, with the result that many real needs may be unnoticed or unappreciated at higher management levels. Experience with the Plan in such a situation suggests that it helps with this problem. Partly help seems to come from the new, more persuasive, and more insistent context in which the branch approaches home base. Partly too, however, operation of the Plan reveals more clearly to people up the line in the organization just exactly what is going on at the work level. With better and more reliable information they can move ahead more confidently with whatever actions seem most appropriate. On the other hand, it is clear that a Plan would fail in the case of a branch plant unable to get decisive action from above, if such action were central to the problems of the branch. The conclusion here, then, is similar to that for the question of size. The Plan does not do away with the difficulties of coordination posed in a large and multiplant company, but, in turn, these difficulties have not made the Plan's operation impossible.

In general, this is the point of view that the parties seem to have developed toward the problems generated by their environments. The Plan has helped them grapple with these problems; in fact the environments have shaped to an important degree the lines of development and principal accomplishments of each situation. The conclusions expressed here are not very different from those of Charles A. Myers, in his review of the studies of peaceful union-management relationships sponsored by the National Planning Association some years ago. As he put his conclusions,[1] "the environmental factors typical of the cases studied are also found in a great many other situations," and a review of various environmental factors "suggests that, in fact, the 'frequently favorable circumstances' are not necessarily and irrevocably fixed. Some are more subject to conscious control than others, but in nearly every one there is a range of possibilities."

The Scanlon Plan, then, has been one important way for the parties to make the best of their environments and, over a period of time, to restructure unfavorable circumstances, such as seasonal fluctuations in employment.

But what about the three or four instances where the Plan has failed or the much larger number of organizations, union and management, who have been told or who have concluded for themselves that they had best not try it? These cases do suggest a few rules of thumb for designating situations where success would be highly unlikely. For the most part, these rules have to do with the attitudes of key individuals and groups rather than the type of environmental circumstance discussed above.

Failure is almost completely predictable when one or possibly both parties see the Plan as a substitute for something else. Suppose some one suggests the Plan as the way out of a collective-bargaining impasse. The company proposes to substitute it for a wage increase or the union wants to "give the Plan to the company" in exchange for some concession. Under these conditions, one or both parties do not really want the Plan with any degree of enthusiasm. Workers are unlikely to put forth critical suggestions and insist that these suggestions be carefully examined, nor is management apt to have thought through and faced up to the Plan's implications for information—sharing and consultation with employees. Success will certainly be unlikely or, at best, difficult to achieve.

Do the parties want the Plan, or do they really want something else, with the Plan a sort of pawn in a larger game? Do the great bulk of the people understand the general ideas involved and actively want to give the Plan a whirl? Answers to these two questions eliminate many who ask for help in establishing a Scanlon Plan.

---

[1] "Fundamentals of Labor Peace: Final Report," *Causes of Industrial Peace Under Collective Bargaining,* National Planning Association, December, 1953, pp. 95 and 96.

Another major problem that may lead to failure arises from indecisiveness on the part of management. We have already touched on the problem as related to the large, complex, multiplant organization. But it exists as well in smaller firms, especially if the structure of ownership is such that there is no agreed center of authority in the firm. The Plan may, of course, make a major contribution to the effectiveness of the firm by forcing management to face up explicitly to the decisions it must make. Failing that, however, the Plan will atrophy. As Joe Scanlon used to put the question, "How hard is it to find the boss?" If that is impossible or very difficult, the Plan is not likely to succeed.

A work force may also be indecisive, of course, and for the same reasons: personal and institutional weakness. If people do not or dare not present and defend their views with vigor, there is little prospect for a successful Plan. This problem makes for difficulty where the firm is non-union or where the local union is weak or badly divided. Factionalism means difficulty for any positive program, and weakness usually means that the tougher and often more unpleasant problems, particularly those that bring out inadequacies or mistakes of management, are unlikely to come to the surface.

Each of the problems outlined here has to do with attitudes rather than physical circumstances beyond anyone's control. Thus the limitations on applicability of the Scanlon Plan seem to be largely the limitations of people. Conversely, success has been achieved in a wide variety of environments, not because these environments were unusually favorable, but because courageous, decisive people found in the Plan a means to meet the varied challenges that face every work group and organization.

ELBRIDGE S. PUCKETT

10 . . . .

Productivity Achievements—
A Measure of Success*

Other chapters in this volume have indicated clearly that productivity achievement is not the only criterion of success of a cooperative effort. The satisfaction of doing a good job, and the development of healthier human relationships and more constructive attitudes toward the changing needs of the business enterprise—these are accomplishments which many participants in the Plan have felt to be most important. Success might be measured by the ability of company and union to understand each other's problems, to be able to sit down and discuss a problem before it becomes a grievance, and to be able to cooperate fully in the area of production without sacrificing their integrity or their institutional obligations.

Much attention has been focused, however, on the productivity increases that have been experienced in Scanlon Plan installations, be-

* The study resulting in this publication was made under a fellowship granted by the Ford Foundation, and the author wishes to acknowledge his indebtedness. However, the conclusions, opinions, and other statements in this publication are those of the author and are not necessarily those of the Ford Foundation.

cause this is one of the more tangible measures of success and because performance is the key not only to bonus earnings but also to the firm's ability to compete in the product market. The purpose of this paper is to discuss the productivity increases that have been achieved in ten situations where the Plan has been used and to evaluate this performance in terms of bonuses earned and savings realized by the firms.

In the first section we will describe the ten situations studied and the variety of environments which are represented in the sample. In the second section we will discuss the use of the Scanlon Plan ratio in evaluating productivity changes and the methods used to control variables which might distort the ratio as a measure of performance. In the third section we will present the results that have been achieved, and in the concluding pages we will evaluate these results in terms of bonuses earned and the impact on the cost structure of the firm.

The Firms Studied

The ten applications of the Scanlon Plan included in this study involve nine firms and eleven plants. One firm applied the Plan separately in two plants, and another firm included two plants under a single measurement. These ten situations were chosen for the study on the basis of the ease with which available data could be translated into reliable estimates of productivity changes. It is believed that these firms offer a representative sample of other situations in which the Plan has been installed, in terms of the wide variety of environments and of the types of problems faced.

Each of the firms operates in a product market that is quite different from the others, although they all are engaged in manufacturing or fabricating of some kind. Three firms produce consumer items, three make producer capital goods, one makes parts which go into consumer goods, and two make finished products which are used in construction or in public institutions. It is interesting that the elasticity of demand facing these firms runs the gamut from very high to quite low. (Although no statistical study could be made of price elasticity, management people involved have expressed their views as to the additional volume of sales that would be available to the firm in relation to various changes in price.) In five of the ten situations it appears that price reduction based on increased efficiency could result in a significant improvement in sales, whereas in the other five cases it appears that price is a less critical determinant of short-run demand.

Employees are represented by no union in one of the ten cases studied, an independent union in one case, and affiliates of national unions in the other eight. The number of employees ranges between 30 in one plant and 1200 in the largest plant. Three plants have fewer than 100 employees, five plants have from 101 to 500 employees, and two plants from 1001 to 1200 employees. There is also a wide variation in labor content (i.e., total payroll as a percentage of the value of production) prior to applying the Plan. One plant has a labor content in the 10 to 12 per cent range, two plants have 21 to 30 per cent, three plants have 31 to 40 per cent, two plants have 41 to 50 per cent, and two plants have labor contents of 51 to 60 per cent.

The mistaken view that the Scanlon Plan has been most often applied in crisis situations is clearly refuted by the firms in this sample. Two of the firms had been exceptionally profitable prior to installing the Scanlon Plan. Three firms had experienced better than average profits relative to other firms in their industry, two had average profitability, one had less than average profitability, and only two of the ten situations were faced with severe financial losses and the possibility of liquidation.

The types of production process vary from mass production and assembly to the job-shop situation. Skills vary from highly skilled machining and toolmaking to low-skilled manual operations. The equipment and machinery varies from the very new and up-to-date plants of three firms to the antiquated and obsolete plant of another. In summary, it can be said that whatever improvements we can document have been achieved under a wide variety of environments and circumstances. The primary similarity that can be identified was that the parties involved in these situations had a strong desire to work together more effectively and were interested in applying the principle of participation.

The Ratio as a Measure of Productivity

In this study physical productivity (i.e., physical output per unit of labor input) is evaluated by comparing the sales value of production in relation to total payroll costs (excluding the Scanlon Plan bonus) in the first two years of operation under the Plan with the ratio of these two variables in the base period. A number of problems are involved in using sales and payroll data as measures of output and labor input, and in most cases the data had to be adjusted to control variables which tend to distort our measure of performance. (For a more thorough elaboration of the components of the Scanlon Plan ratio, see the earlier article in this volume entitled "Measuring Performance under the Scanlon Plan" by the present author.)

The first control which was exercised was to choose from a larger sample of firms which might have been studied only those firms which had not experienced unmanageable changes in the control variables. The selection of the time period which was studied was also designed to minimize changes in the control variables which would accumulate over a longer period of time. This choice of time period also tends to catch firms at different stages of the business cycle, since these firms installed the Plan at different times over the past seven years. Finally, the base-period ratio of sales value of production to total payroll has been adjusted to eliminate the separate effects on the ratio of changes in prices, wages, technology, product mix, new products, fixed elements in the work force, overtime hours, and "farmed-out" work brought back to the plant.

In every situation except one the base period covered one full year, a period which was long enough to include the seasonal fluctuations which are inherent in the business. In the exceptional case a base period of a year and one-half was required to include a complete cycle of the business.

Productivity Achievements

In the table efficiency in the ten situations is expressed as a percentage of the efficiency in the base period. As each year normally reflects the seasonal fluctuations, the performance is shown for each year separately in columns 1 and 2, and the two years are averaged in column 3 to arrive at the performance for the total period studied.

It will be noted that for each company the average of the two-year performance is not weighted by the volume of sales or production, but each year is treated as an integral unit. It may be argued with good logic that a weighted average would be more representative of the performance in the two-year period. In each case, however, this would tend to raise the averages in column 3, because it would give heavier weight to the year in which production was highest. Thus, the only defense for using unweighted averages is that it yields the more conservative result. When discussing the average productivity increase for all ten firms, however, it would not be meaningful to weight the average by size, sales, or payroll. In this context we are interested only in getting a picture of what ten production units have accomplished, regardless of size or other characteristics.

In the first year under the Plan, productivity increased 6.8 per cent

Percentage Increases in Productivity

Company	First-Year Relative Efficiency	Second-Year Relative Efficiency	Two-Year Average Relative Efficiency (Unweighted)
	(1)	(2)	(3)
A	14.9	10.9	12.9
B	21.9	12.7	17.3
C	16.7	13.2	15.0
D	36.7	29.3	33.0
E	28.9	49.4	39.2
F	32.9	42.9	37.9
G	38.7	25.1	31.9
H	14.1	16.5	15.3
I	12.9	23.2	18.1
J	6.8	13.7	10.3
Average (Unweighted)	22.5	23.7	23.1

in the lowest case and 38.7 per cent in the highest, with an average improvement of 22.5 per cent for the group as a whole. In the second year, improvement ranged between 10.9 per cent and 49.4 per cent, with an average gain of 23.7 per cent. For the two-year period, 10.3 per cent was the minimum improvement and 39.2 per cent the maximum, with an average of 23.1 per cent resulting in the ten situations.

An analysis of the magnitude of productivity gains in relation to environmental factors yields no positive relationships that can be identified. It is interesting that of the four firms that achieved improvements in excess of 30 per cent, only one had previously faced serious financial problems, and the other three firms had experienced profits that were better than average for their industries. This suggests that such productivity gains can be achieved in the absence of the motivation of job salvation. If we can assume that better than average profitability is indicative of better than average efficiency, these data also suggest that there is plenty of room for improvement in firms which are already relatively efficient.

Size of firm does not appear to be a controlling factor in the results. The two largest firms both experienced productivity gains equal to the average for all the firms studied. The experience of these firms indicates that it requires hard work and effective leadership to achieve success. However, the people in these situations contend that it requires, in any event, good leadership to operate a plant with 1000 or more employees, and the Scanlon Plan makes the job much easier in view of improved communications, better understanding, and ease of implementing decisions. Therefore, it would appear that the contention that the Scanlon Plan is limited to small firms needs further consideration.

As only one firm in the sample has no union, and one firm involves an independent union, it is impossible to say whether or not unionization is a necessary ingredient for success under the Plan. Joe Scanlon feared that where a strong union was not at hand, workers would be afraid to voice their criticism of management decisions and would be prone to use the production committees for grievances and bargaining problems which are normally processed by the union. Although the non-union situation experienced somewhat less than average increase in productivity, both it and the situation involving the independent union have been leaders in terms of the number of accepted suggestions submitted per employee.

A view that is quite often expressed is that the greater the labor content, the easier it is to improve labor productivity, that is, the more "room" there is to move in. The experience in these ten situations, however, certainly belies this contention. Three of the four firms which achieved the greatest productivity gains have labor contents of less than 35 per cent of their sales value of production. The firm with the lowest content (less than 20 per cent) increased its productivity as much as the average of the ten firms studied. The only conclusion that can be supported by the data is that labor content varies widely from one product to another and from one operation to another and is not necessarily a sign of good or poor efficiency. Regardless of labor content, judging from these firms, there was a reservoir of ideas and capability that responded to the challenge of participation.

Productivity increases do not appear related to the type of production process or the type of product involved. The job shop fared well in comparison with the mass-producer. The relatively low-skilled operations compared well with the highly skilled; the companies with old equipment compared well with the best equipped firms.

The type of product involved does not seem to have enhanced the productivity potential. The product market does influence the situation to the extent that substantial shifts in product demand can disrupt the organization in many ways. A sharp drop in demand makes it more difficult to maintain a steady flow of work through the shop. The psychological pitch of the work force is necessarily at a lower key when the challenge of a heavy schedule is lacking. Most of these firms have attempted to avert layoffs and keep the team together whenever possible by shifting production workers to maintenance of plant and equipment. This necessarily shows up as a decline in efficiency in terms of the variables used in the study. The introduction of new products involves expensive manufacturing operations until new equipment is available and the kinks worked out of new processes.

These and many other problems affect the performance in every situation. The increases in productivity from the first to the second year in five cases and the decrease in productivity experienced in the other five cases appear to be attributable largely to these types of external forces, rather than to any increase or diminution of enthusiasm in the cooperative effort. A conclusion that is surprising to many people is that sharp increases in productivity can and have been accomplished almost immediately after the Plan is installed. Although it may require some time for the full effect of suggestions to be felt, the change in attitude and a new *esprit de corps* seem to be vital factors in the rapid attainment of better performance.

Thus, in our experience there is no necessary reason to expect that the second year under the Plan should be more fruitful than the first. On the other hand, there is no suggestion in the data that enthusiasm must wane after the first challenges are met and conquered. In a dynamic society, new products, new processes, and new problems are always arising to offer new challenges. This view is supported by reports from firms which have had the Plan for several years. Even the plants which have been outstanding in terms of both productivity and suggestions in the first two years find that there is room for additional gains in performance and that the quantity and quality of suggestions can be maintained.

The only variables which seem to be prerequisites for success under the Scanlon Plan are leadership, sincerity, and the desire to participate in a more cooperative and productive relationship. Where these ingredients are present, significant productivity increases have been achieved without regard for the environment or circumstances.

Bonus and Cost Implications

In each of the ten situations studied, 75 per cent of the labor savings is shared by participants in the Plan and 25 per cent is retained by the company. This means that on the average employees in these firms earned in bonus approximately 17.4 per cent of their gross pay during the two-year period. Employees in the firm which experienced a 10.3 per cent improvement would have earned approximately a 7.7 per cent bonus. In the plant where productivity went up 39.2 per cent, bonuses would have averaged about 29.4 per cent.

These figures, however, do not express the full impact of their achievements. Almost invariably, the firms have improved their competitive position in the product market, which has helped to make jobs more secure. In none of the firms studied has employment declined, and in most cases it has increased. Through their cooperative efforts, attempts have been made to stabilize employment over the course of business fluctuations.

To illustrate the labor savings experienced by the firms, let us assume (to use round figures) that the average productivity increase amounted to 20 per cent. If the base-period labor cost in a particular firm were 24 per cent of the sales value of production, a 20 per cent improvement would yield a new labor ratio of 20 per cent (i.e., 24 ÷ 1.2) and a bonus pool of 4 per cent of the sales value of production. After paying out 75 per cent of this pool in bonus, the company's savings in labor costs would equal 1 per cent of the sales value of production. If the company's base-period labor costs were instead 48 per cent of the sales value of production, the above figures would of course be doubled.

This analysis does not include savings that may be realized through the better utilization of materials, supplies, equipment, and tools. A number of companies have found that capital requirements have been reduced when a more rapid production cycle permits the reduction of inventories. Others have indicated that they have felt the greatest impact in terms of improved quality and promptness in meeting delivery schedules. These improvements are impossible to measure in dollars and cents, but are felt by company and employees in the form of increased sales to satisfied customers.

Conclusion

In this study we have attempted to measure the productivity achieved in a representative sample of firms operating under the Scanlon Plan. As in any study of productivity, the data are by no means exact, but they do yield an approximate indication of the magnitude of productivity gains that have been realized.

In this writer's view the most significant conclusion to be drawn from the study is not that productivity achievements have been substantial, although this too is important. The most significant conclusion suggested in these data is that our human resources contain a potential that is apparently not fully utilized in even relatively efficient and profitable manufacturing companies. To tap this reservoir of human potential is the great challenge facing labor-management relations today.

CLINTON S. GOLDEN

11 . . . .

The Significance of Labor-
Management Cooperation

It is always stimulating to attend Scanlon Plan conferences at M.I.T. because of the extraordinary demonstrated willingness of those who have had fruitful experiences with the operation of the Scanlon Plan to share their knowledge and experience with those seeking to achieve a more harmonious and creative relationship.

So in this spirit of sharing I want to share with you some of my own thoughts and observations concerning the climate and quality of relationships between those classified as employees and their employers and their management representatives. What I shall have to say derives mainly from my own personal experiences and observations as an employee in earlier years; as a labor-organization member and officer and more recently as an adviser or consultant to both unions and corporate management.

First I want to assert that man is by nature essentially a cooperative, rather than a combative, competitive, predatory creature. In other words, he is a social being—one who is basically concerned not with himself alone but with his fellows. To me there is no more dramatic evidence of this than his capacity to associate with his fellows in an infinite variety of ways for the attainment of common or acceptable goals that cannot be achieved purely by his own efforts.

This capacity for association—for cooperative effort—is not by any means a new or recent phenomenon. It has been evident throughout most of recorded history. In the primitive societies of the early pre-Christian era when the sole source of energy was the muscular power of human beings kept in bondage there is—thanks to the explorations and researches of archeologists and other scholars—abundant evidence of the existence of associations—primitive to be sure—that were formed by the slaves or bondsmen of that period to secure and share food with their fellows, to bury their dead, and indeed to struggle together to attain freedom from bondage and despotism and achieve a better life.

The guilds of masters, artisans, and craftsmen in the Middle Ages are another example of this continuing capacity for association. The so-called Friendly Societies which first appeared in England at the beginning of the Industrial Revolution are a later example. And finally today the modern trade or industrial union is a manifestation of this same capacity. Time does not permit reciting in detail the contributions that these organizations of lowly and humble people have made in the age-old struggle of man for freedom and a fuller life. We may observe, however, that they have played an important role in developing newer and higher concepts of man's relations with his fellows.

We presently live in this country, at least, in an age of organization. It is organization rather than the genius and effort of the individual that makes modern production and distribution possible. We are all aware of the tremendous achievements of corporate organizations that bring together capital, expensive equipment, technical administrative skills, and the work force. We have not in the main, however, concerned ourselves extensively with the psychological effect of advancing industrialization on the individual and the groups who compromise the corporate organization in its entirety.

"In other fields," says Professor William Foote Whyte in his thorough case study of union-management relations in one plant, "the American businessman is a brilliant experimenter. He is quick to try new machines and processes, new job methods and production layouts, new merchandising and advertising methods, etc. But this ingenuity is often discarded when he enters the field of labor relations. There he seems to seek out the security of the old ways of doing things." However, "events force him to change. But all too often he changes reluctantly, and so is unable to capitalize on new situations."

This, of course, is a general observation. There are significant exceptions. Those from industry and labor who are participating in this conference are among the notable exceptions. When it comes to discovering new and better relations among those employed in the workplace, it is those who have the imagination, vision, and courage to deviate from familiar paths that make the really significant contributions. They are the innovators rather than the standpatters.

There are others in widely separated parts of the world who are seeking new approaches in industrial relations which have recently been brought to my attention. Within the past two weeks I have had inquiries from educators and industrialists in such distant lands as Holland and Chile for information concerning the content and objectives of the Scanlon Plan.

In response to these and other inquiries that periodically come to me, I am obliged to reply that it is not a "plan" if by that is meant a formula, blueprint, or design that can be taken out of the files and applied to almost any situation. Rather, I am obliged to say, it is an idea which, under certain circumstances and conditions, can be embraced by both management and labor to their mutual economic advantage and satisfaction.

This idea begins with a recognition of the fact that a normal individual performing an assigned task for a considerable period of time will generally acquire a greater knowledge of the nature of that task than is possessed by any other person. In effect this assigned task in time becomes a part of his way of life, for upon it or some other task his life and well-being depend.

In the performance of that task the individual can experience happiness and sense of achievement, or defeat and frustration. Most individuals want to be happy in their work. They want to feel that they are individually useful and necessary in relation to the orderly and successful operation of the enterprise in which they are employed.

In the course of work experience the individual instinctively gives much thought to what he is doing. If the task is unduly burdensome, he thinks about how it may be made less so. If it is repetitive and monotonous, he thinks of ways of making it more interesting. If he has an inventive turn of mind, he thinks of ways of improving the efficiency of his own and related operations. At the same time he seeks the friendly fellowship of his co-workers.

It may be argued that there is no readily available scientific evidence to support these assertions concerning the actual or potential work or job interests of the individual workers. I think the evidence is there for those who care to collect and examine it. Some of it will be available in the course of this conference as the participants relate their own experiences.

I spoke of an instinctive interest on the part of the worker in his work. That, in part, is a heritage or carry-over from the past. In the simple handicraft stage of production there existed every reason for such interest because the worker possessed certain craft or artisan skills, owned his own tools, and derived his livelihood pretty directly from the sale of the products he created. His income, upon which his own well-being and that of his family depended, was made possible by the application of his skills and the economical and efficient use of materials together with the quality and usefulness of his product.

In the complex organization of modern production the old craft and artisan skills have been extensively diluted by the division of labor and specialization of tasks. The personally owned handicraft tools have been replaced by the power-driven tools and machines provided by the funds of investors who are personally unknown to the individual worker. The task to which he has been assigned was devised and outlined by some unknown person in the mass-production organization. Frequently the worker has little if any knowledge of the relation of his task to a given end product. He is expected to do as he is told and is usually *not* required to do any creative thinking. The whole organization of production is so impersonal as to leave little opportunity for creative personal expression or the assumption of personal responsibility.

Personal pride in workmanship and responsible work performance have been replaced by greater interest in required hours of work, quitting time, pay day, and what to do with leisure time. Complicated individual incentives impersonally devised and designed to spur the worker on to ever greater output probably produce more problems of relations and other problems and costs than they are worth. All serve to discourage and stifle individual initiative and retard natural creative interest in work and workplace associations.

Certainly the variety and volume of industrial production requires cooperative effort on the part of individuals and groups. But how is it achieved? Through fear of loss of jobs in a surplus labor market? By compulsions of one kind or another—subtle and not so subtle? Or by voluntary action and effort on the part of eager and willing individual participants in a common endeavor?

Let me turn at this point to certain moral considerations. We live in a society deeply devoted in principle to recognition of the worth and dignity of the human personality. We believe that government derives its just powers from the *consent* of the governed and that the "pursuit of happiness" is the basic right of every individual. On the moral foundation created by these principles we have erected a structure of political democracy in which every adult citizen has an equal opportunity for participation. It is of course true that not *every* citizen *avails* himself of the opportunity for participation in political affairs. But the opportunity to do so exists and is jealously safeguarded.

Let me turn briefly to the modern industrial enterprise functioning within the framework of our political democracy. Here we see assembled as employees, or citizens, if you please, men and women of varied occupational interests, talents, and abilities. Because modern production is the result of organized effort and direction rather than of isolated individual performance, what amounts to a new type of community has come into being. This community corresponds to the industrial workplace rather than to a geographical area or a defined political subdivision. Because of the nature of its evolution and development, it has been managed or governed by autocratic rather than democratic principles and procedures.

To be sure, traditional autocratic industrial-management practices have been modified to some extent by the emergence of unions and the introduction of collective-bargaining procedures. Where unions exist and have established a contractual relationship with the management of the enterprise, managerial policies and decisions are subject to review and modifications under certain conditions. Unions are thus placed in the position of being what amounts to a party of opposition with a negative, rather than a positive, approach to the problems of managing or governing the workplace community.

There is no doubt in my mind that the most effective appeal that the union organization can offer to the non-union workers is that of opportunity for personal participation in the affairs of the union which are of necessity related to the affairs of the enterprise in which its members are employed. It is here that the central point of the Scanlon Plan attains significance.

We live in an age of organization. Within the organization of the enterprise the organization of the workers must function if it is to be useful and meaningful to them. The fact that it can function negatively as a party of opposition to management is well established. But the fact that the union can maintain its institutional integrity and sovereignty and perform a positive and constructive role is a comparatively new development which can be largely credited to the vision and initiative of people who are participating in this conference. Whether or not the area in which this kind of performance expands will depend in large part on management's vision, courage, and leadership qualities.

Where such initiative and leadership qualities have been displayed the union has gradually assumed a new and constructive role. It becomes the instrumentality which has served to unlock the storehouse of work experience of the individual members and release the accumulated ideas, resources, and ingenuity that have seldom been encouraged to find expression or application.

It is thus that what amounts to a new way of life begins to take form. The worker becomes a full adult citizen instead of an impersonal subject of managerial authority in the workplace community. As opportunities for participation open up in the new environment of relations, as he gains the recognition, prestige, and status that normal persons seek, his self-confidence and self-respect increase. His frustrations disappear, and his employment—his job—becomes more meaningful. His desire for self-fulfillment begins to be satisfied.

You may say that I have been talking chiefly about psychological responses and matters related to the human spirit. What about the concrete benefits and material rewards that may legitimately be expected to flow from the somewhat utopian industrial workplace community you have been talking about?

In response to this question I must first remind you that "man does not live by bread alone." Bread is important to be sure, for it sustains life. It was not the expectation of financial remuneration alone that motivated union steelworkers when they challenged the management of one company to name its most efficient and productive department and then proceeded to increase production in it by 210 per cent.

It is not solely the expectation of higher take-home pay that impels union employees of the Lapointe Machine Tool Company, which is represented in this conference, to share freely their intimate personal knowledge of work methods and processes with both management and newly hired employees in the interest of more efficient operations. In these and a growing number of other instances, management has been rewarded for its part in creating a new environment of relations by increased output, better products, lower unit costs, and, perhaps more importantly, by peace of mind, good will, and decent fellowship with the work force.

The great growth in union membership and influence in the past decade necessitates a fresh look at the industrial-relations scene. I fear that, for the most part, management looks upon unions as unwanted intruders in the enterprise. That they are capable of becoming constructive participants is being demonstrated daily now by Fred Lesieur who is carrying on Joe Scanlon's work with his colleagues here at M.I.T.

I think the time has come for management to decide whether it wants to maintain the status quo or to begin the charting of new courses in the largely unexplored areas of human relations in the industrial workplaces of our nation. It is my firm conviction that rich rewards await those prepared to raise their sights and move forward. There are unfinished tasks of great magnitude ahead of us. Once our nation has attained a position of adequate defense strength and we pass the peak of government defense spending, new problems of adjustment to the requirements of peacetime production and distribution will confront us. I want to close with quotations from two thoughtful people that well deserve repeating.

The first is from that stimulating and provocative book, *The New Society*, by Peter Drucker. He says,

To be productive and efficient, the enterprise needs the abilities, initiative and co-operation of every member more than any previous system of production. Its human resources are its greatest asset—and the one least used. . . . The major incentives to productivity and efficiency are social and moral rather than financial.

At a postwar convention of the National Association of Manufacturers, Clarence Francis, Chairman of the Board of the General Foods Corporation, delivered a remarkable address in the course of which he said:

You can buy a man's time, you can buy a man's physical presence at a given place; you can even buy a measured number of skilled muscular motions per day or per hour. But you cannot buy enthusiasm . . . initiative . . . loyalty; you cannot buy the devotion of hearts, minds and souls. You have to earn these things.

It is ironic that Americans—the most advanced people technically, mechanically, and industrially—should have waited until a comparatively recent period to inquire into the most promising single source of productivity: namely, the human will to work. It is hopeful, on the other hand, that the search is now under way.

APPENDIXES . . . . .

APPENDIX A..

Sample Memorandum
of Understanding
and Sample Suggestions

The following sample memorandum of understanding is a composite of agreements reached by several companies and unions which have successfully applied the principles of the Scanlon Plan to their operations. As such, it covers the usual problems which arise at the inception of the Plan. It is intended to serve as a guide rather than as a rigid formula in dealing with these problems. The special circumstances of a case, or new insights into the issues dealt with, might call for departure from this sample procedure.

MEMORANDUM OF UNDERSTANDING
between

_____
(company)

and

_____
(union)

This agreement is a supplement to the basic labor agreement between the company and the union, and can in no way invalidate or conflict with any of the provisions therein.

I. Plant-Wide Incentive Plan

This memorandum of understanding establishes a plant-wide incentive plan designed to enable all employees and officers of the ———————— Company, up to and including the President, to benefit from their increased cooperation and efforts as reflected in increased productivity.

In order to assure full participation in the benefits of the increased productivity which should result from the employee-management cooperation plan, a plant-wide monthly productivity bonus shall be applied, effective

———————— 19—, to remain in full force and effect for a trial period of one year, after which time its continuance will be subject to the approval of both the management and the union.

II. Basis of the Plan

The Productivity Ratio

The ratio of payroll costs to sales value of production is the base used for the participating productivity bonus. Sales value of production includes gross sales, less returns in each month, plus or minus inventory change in finished goods and work in process. Records for the twelve-month period ending ———————— 19—, were used in

the development of a ratio of (say) 44.06 cents in payroll costs to each dollar in production value. Therefore in each month —— per cent of each dollar of production value will represent the allowed payroll cost. Whenever the actual monthly payroll is less than the allowed pay-

roll, the difference will constitute the bonus pool. However, in order to protect the company's interest in any month when the actual payroll exceeds the allowed, caus-

ing a deficit, a reserve will be accumulated in months when bonuses are earned. For this purpose 25 per cent of the bonus pool will be set aside. If this reserve fund should, in twelve months' time, exceed the amount required to restore the ratio to the established norm in the deficit months, the excess shall then be distributed as

a "year-end bonus," to be shared in the same manner as the monthly bonus. If the deficits for the Scanlon Plan trial period exceed the amount in the reserve fund, this deficit shall be terminated at the end of the Scanlon

Plan trial period and shall not be charged against any bonus earnings of the next year.

After the reserve has been set aside, the balance of the bonus pool shall be divided, with 75 per cent going to the participants and 25 per cent being retained by the company.

75–25 split

In calculating the distribution of the participating employees' portion, their aggregate share will appear as a certain percentage of their total earnings for the month. This percentage will indicate the bonus earnings of each participant. As required by fair labor standards legislation, total earnings for the month will include all straight time hourly earnings and any shift bonuses and/or overtime premia paid. For purposes of bonus distribution, however, total earnings will *not* include the following: (1) earnings of new employees who have not yet been in the employ of the company for 30 days; (2) lost-time earnings of employees whose pay goes on while they are sick or absent for personal reasons; (3) vacation and holiday pay.

participating payroll

The productivity bonus ratio is derived from the record of performance for the twelve-month period ending ———————, 19—. Substantial changes in the conditions which prevailed (with respect to such variables as wages, prices, product mix, technology, etc.) in establishing the ratio may necessitate changing this ratio in order to protect the equity of either party. Accounting practices and procedures may ascertain the adjustment to be made.

basis for ratio change

A general increase or decrease in either wages or selling price may disturb the relationship of payroll to sales, requiring a review and possibly an adjustment of the basic ratio. Similarly, substantial fluctuations in the product mix, with its various labor content proportions, may create inequities requiring a ratio revision.

prices, wages, product mix

The Plan is designed to compensate all employees for their ideas and efforts. Technological change requiring capital expenditures may alter the ratio by reducing labor costs without any increase in productive efficiency on the part of the participants. It is understood that in the event the employee representatives suggest mechanical changes which eliminate a job or jobs, the employees and the company will meet and make an earnest effort to place the employees affected on other jobs.

placing employees

Any substantial influence not brought about by an increase or decrease in productive efficiency will furnish sufficient reason for an over-all survey of the presently established ratio. However, not every change in the variables affecting the ratio should require ratio adjustment, since the development of the ratio itself reflects certain fluctuations which prevailed in the base period with respect to wage structure, labor turnover, product mix, price policy, etc.

III. The Committee Structure

The heart of this plant-wide incentive plan is participation, implemented by the creation of joint committees of management and employees to promote increased productive efficiency. The committee structure includes production committees and a screening committee.

Production Committees

There shall be a production committee established for each of the following plant divisions or departments:

_____

_____

_____

_____

COMPOSITION

Production committees shall be each composed of _____ management and _____ union representatives. Union representatives chosen in the first election shall serve for the trial period of the Plan, at the end of which term a definite elective period will be determined.

FUNCTIONS

The production committees shall meet in their divisions at least once each month, or more often if deemed necessary, for the specific purpose of discussing ways and means of reducing waste and increasing productive efficiency. Every effort will be made to schedule in advance of such meeting a specific production problem which will be placed on the agenda for discussion. Committee members may call upon those employees in their division who are most familiar with the specific problem outlined to participate in the scheduled meetings. In no event, however, may a committeeman call in more than *two* employees. It shall be the responsibility of the production committeemen to record and explain all suggestions intended to increase productive efficiency or reduce waste, which are made to them by the employees in their division.

The production committees shall keep accurate minutes of their meetings showing all suggestions designed to increase productive efficiency or reduce waste together with their disposition of the same. An approved copy of the minutes shall be transmitted immediately to the screening committee.

The functions of the production committees shall in no way conflict with the responsibilities and duties of the duly elected grievance committees. The grievance committeeman may, if he deems it advisable, attend all meetings of the production committee conducted in his department or the unit to which he belongs.

The Screening Committee

COMPOSITION

The screening committee shall consist of ——————— management and a like number of union representatives, these members to be appointed or elected by their constituents.

FUNCTIONS

This committee shall screen out through joint discussion all suggestions that are designed to increase productive efficiency or reduce waste. Those that have been placed in effect at the production-committee level shall be placed in the record, and decisions shall be reached concerning those suggestions which have not been disposed of at the production committee level.

It will also be the function of this committee to go over the facts and figures used in the calculation of the bonus for the previous month before it is announced, in order to establish the greatest degree of faith and confidence in the calculated results. The productive efficiency bonus will be announced on or before the —————— day of each month and will represent the bonus for the previous month.

Method of Bonus Calculation and Distribution

1. Assume that in the 12-month base period the payroll cost of making each dollar's worth of production value was 44.06 cents.

This establishes a *productivity norm* or ratio of 44.06 per cent against which to measure your performance each month:

For Example

2. Assume that in this month the *sales value of production* comes to $87,837.00
3. If performance had been no better this month than the average for the base period, the payroll would have come to $38,701.00

This is your *allowed payroll*.
(44.06 × 87,837)

4. Say the actual payroll for this month, however, figured out to $30,985.00
5. This would mean an improvement over the norm amounting to .... $ 7,716.00

This is your *BONUS POOL*.

6. Now set aside 25 per cent of this, or .... $ 1,929.00
   as a *reserve*.
7. Which leaves *for immediate distribution* the sum of $ 5,787.00
8. Deduct the company's share (25 per cent) .... $ 1,447.00
9. And the employees' share (75 per cent) is .... $ 4,340.00
10. This share for the employees is 14.0%
    of the actual payroll.

This is your *bonus percentage paid*.
(4,340 + 30,985.00)

11. Suppose your own pay record for this month looked like this:

Name	Total Hours Worked	Including Overtime Hours	Hourly Rate	Total Pay	Bonus Per Cent	Bonus	Total
John Doe	200	40	1.50	$330.00	14.0	46.20	$376.20

Employee Suggestions under the Scanlon Plan

The following is a selection of suggestions made by employees in representative industries which operate under the principles and procedures of the Scanlon Plan.

Auto Parts Industry

1. Change shield die to use up 1¾-inch steel which was scrapped last year. The die was made to use 2-inch steel. Using the 1¾-inch steel will save 4000 pounds of steel.

This suggestion was put into effect and resulted in a saving to the company of 4000 pounds of steel.

2. The following suggestion pertains to the clock-winding mechanism or clock motor as we call it.

From the coil which is mounted on the motor plate, a wire of approximately 1 inch in length leads to an insulated terminal on the plate where it is staked. The original design of the motor provided for spaghetti-type insulation to be placed on this length of wire prior to staking, which very measurably slowed production and increased costs and, of course, the insulating material itself was a cost factor.

This suggestion to eliminate the insulator and speed up the job was originally rejected by the engineering department as electrically unsound, but due to persistent employee action and engineering department cooperation, a method was found to bring about the change with a resultant saving of about $10,000 per year. A substantial part of this saving accrues directly to the company in the form of material saving.

3. This suggestion is aimed at what has been the biggest problem in the punch-press department. There are some thirty presses in everyday use which are hand-fed, and compressed air is used to blow the parts off the die into a suitable container in back of the press. We have a high volume of this type of operation and the handling of parts without damage has always been a problem.

The suggestion is to make a simple chute which can easily be fastened to the back of the press which would facilitate passing the parts from the press to the container. Such a chute was made by the suggestors and adapted to the thirty presses. Although we cannot say exactly how many dollars have been saved, these chutes have saved a great deal of setup time, which means more production, and damaged parts have been greatly reduced.

Pen and Pencil Industry

4. I suggest that we wrap cotton on the bottom of the rotary brushes making it possible to wipe the inside end of collector shells in one operation.

When the suggestion was implemented, it became possible for the operator to do the two operations in half the previous time.

5. This is a suggestion to add one more arbor to the Porter cable dial. As there were seven arbors in use before, the additional arbor increases production by over 14 per cent on each machine, and the volume of work on this job is very large.

6. Put a Syntron Hopper feed on Cincinnati grinders for erasers. This cuts about 98 per cent of the manual labor out of this operation.

Shoe Industry

7. At present, we use No. 1, 2, and 3 Littleway saddles, No. 1 and 2 welt saddles, left and right, branded and unbranded, which means 20 boxes plus special saddles. If we had a set of dies to be used on either right or left foot, we could reduce the number by one half and make the handling much easier and faster for the operator.

Steel Fabricating

8. It is suggested that one sandblast operation be eliminated on machine manhole collars 24-inch diameter and larger. The present routing for these collars is to sandblast, magnaflux, and stock. When issued from the stock, the collars first go to sandblast, then to the fabrication department, after welding them onto the tank, the tank is sandblasted.

It was agreed that in the future the collars could be sent directly from the stockroom to the fabrication department, thus eliminating that particular sandblast operation.

Machine Tool Industry

9. A worker thought the process in grinding round broaches could be done in less time. The procedure in use was to start the machine, grind off a little stock, press the stop button, wait for the machine to coast to a stop, and then "mike" the broach. This particular worker thought there was too long a wait between pressing the stop button and being able to mike the broach. He had the idea that applying some kind of electrical brake on the machine would make it stop faster and therefore speed up production.

After discussing the idea with the foreman and electrician, a practical solution was worked out. The results, as told by the electrician, were:

This didn't require a major change in the machine, because we found a way of supplying a source of d.c. current directly to the motor windings and using a shot of d.c. current as a brake. The time saved was so great that, after we put it on the first one, they applied it to seventeen machines.

They tell me this saves one hour a day per machine. It costs only $1.25 for the fuse block, about $14.00 for the relay, plus a couple of hours of the maintenance man to install.

Wood Products

10. It was suggested that a conveyor chain be installed on the infeed side of the incisor. This would bring the cross tie to the man rather than the man hauling the tie to the roll conveyor. This suggestion was put into effect at nominal cost with a consequent production increase of approximately 30 per cent.

11. It is suggested that a track liner be purchased at a cost of $38.00, and the production on this operation was increased by 100 per cent.

JOSEPH N. SCANLON

APPENDIX B . .

Profit Sharing under
Collective Bargaining:
Three Case Studies

In the postwar period of labor unrest considerable attention has been focused on profit-sharing plans as a remedy for current industrial relations ills. Proponents of the idea insist that strikes and low productivity are twin symptoms of an internal maladjustment. The real trouble, they say, lies in the worker's fear of insecurity and his belief that he is being exploited. The solution, so runs the argument, is to hitch the wage earner's interest to the employer's profits. Both thereafter will work together in peace and harmony. And, indeed, this has been the experience in isolated cases; but most schemes have been far less successful. They have failed to show even the most elementary common sense in devising means to create greater worker interest in the welfare of the enterprise.

In a quick check of its records the National Industrial Conference Board reports that of 161 profit-sharing plans surveyed in 1937, about 60 per cent had been abandoned. The Board warned employers

Reprinted by permission from the October, 1948, issue of *Industrial and Labor Relations Review.*

against too quick judgment on the advisability of following the profit-sharing movement.

Nevertheless, profit-sharing plans seem more tempting today than ever before. The reason is simple. Since V-J Day, the wage issue has all but erased other questions affecting labor and management. Union statisticians charge that since the war real wages have fallen while profits have soared. Management, on the other hand, answers, "Yes, we're making money, but with our costs so high, even a small drop in demand can put us in the red." Profit sharing, then, is thought of as a substitute for a wage increase. And while no national policy has as yet been adopted, unions in general have opposed profit-sharing plans because they have been used as a substitute for a justifiable wage increase—a substitute which amounted to a wage increase with a re-triever string attached.

Labor also has a historical objection to profit sharing. Too often in the past a plan of this kind was introduced as a weapon to combat union organization. And even when this was not the ulterior purpose, the effect upon the minds of the employees was the same, for management conceived and established such plans on a unilateral basis. Quite naturally, union membership viewed with hostility and suspicion a program which weakened the principles of collective bargaining. And in by-passing representatives of the employees, management failed to develop a sense of partnership or participation, indispensable ingredients to the fulfillment of any program to foster greater productive efficiency.

The following case histories of three profit-sharing plans, one a complete success, the other two failures, may well point up the strength and weaknesses inherent in the basic idea, together with some important elements which influence the broad over-all results.

Profit-Sharing Plan Number 1

Case History no. 1	Failure
Company A	Basic steel industry
Employees	1600
1. Union affiliation	C.I.O.—first agreement 1945
2. Type of labor agreement	Standard
3. Institution of profit-sharing plan	1939
4. Method of application	Fixed amount—5 cents per hour per employee
5. Type of payment	Lump sum, once a year
6. Company's financial position	Good, consistent profit maker

In 1936 when the organizing drives were instituted in the mass-production industries, the employer already had a well-developed program designed to combat outside organization of his employees. It followed the usual pattern. A company union was set up and functioning. There is little doubt that the company was entirely responsible for this development. Through the company union the employees had been granted all of the advantages in wages, hours, and working conditions gained through collective bargaining processes by the Steelworkers' Organizing Committee in the plants that had been organized.

Nevertheless, early in 1938 an organizing drive conducted by the Steelworkers' Organizing Committee seemed destined to succeed, and they petitioned the National Labor Relations Board for an election. At this juncture the company decided to install a profit-sharing plan. The proposal presented to the company union officials contained the following provisions:

A. If the board of directors decided at their first meeting after the end of each fiscal year that the company had enjoyed a good year, then each employee of the company would share in the profits of the preceding year.

B. Each employee currently employed would receive a bonus of five cents per hour for each hour worked during the preceding year.

C. This agreement would remain in effect only so long as the present bargaining agent represented the employees. In the event of a change in representation, the plan was automatically canceled.

This agreement proved to be a most effective weapon in combating outside organization. In the National Labor Relations Board election, the employees voted overwhelmingly to continue the company union. They reasoned that if they could secure an increase of 5 cents an hour over and above that being paid in all other basic steel plants in the area, this was more than they could expect to accomplish in a monetary way if they were represented by the Steelworkers' Union.

Beginning with 1938, for six consecutive years the bonus was paid. The employees were well aware of the fact that they were receiving this bonus for staying out of the union. Just as regularly, each year prior to the meeting of the Board of Directors a synthetic organizing threat developed within the ranks of the employees. Pamphlets were distributed and organizers were called in to address meetings. A great deal of excitement was generated. "If you join an outside union," the workers were told, "you will lose your bonus." This pressure campaign never failed to achieve the desired objective. The board of directors always decided that the company had experienced a good year and the bonus was paid. During six years of operation the company had paid out approximately $1,250,000 in bonuses and had received in return the somewhat dubious satisfaction of keeping the union out. No sense of partnership, no joint participation in an effort to increase efficiency, no effort to improve the profit-making possibilities or the competitive position of the company had been developed. The plan was founded on hypocrisy and bad faith and had degenerated into a subtle game of wits.

Early in 1945 the United Steelworkers of America (the old S.W.O.C.) conducted an intensive drive at the properties of the company. It proved successful. A majority of the employees voted in an N.L.R.B. election for the Steelworkers' Union, despite the fact that the company again used the bonus elimination threat as its chief weapon. The union had made a sizable wage demand on the industry, and it dwarfed the importance of the 5 cent per hour bonus or share of the profits.

The industry refused to grant the demands of the union, and a strike ensued. The employees of this company joined in the work stoppage. Agreement was finally reached on the basic wage issue with 95 per cent of the industry, and the employees returned to work. Not so with this company. The strike here was continued for several additional weeks. The profit-sharing bonus was the stumbling block that prevented a settlement. The company was willing to grant the 18.5 cent per hour wage increase, but insisted that the plan must be discontinued. The union contended that wage stabilization was in effect and that the profit-sharing bonus could not be canceled. It had been paid during the entire period of wage stabilization and now was considered a part of the wage structure. The O.P.A. had granted the industry price increases to compensate them fully for the general wage increase over their previously existing wage structure.

A compromise settlement was finally reached on the following basis: The profit-sharing plan was continued as originally applied with 5 cents per hour for each hour worked by every employee during the year. The profits after taxes of the second lowest year beginning with 1938 through 1944 were used as the base to determine whether the bonus was payable. This base replaced the original understanding, which left the matter to the decision of the board of directors. Likewise, it took the issue out of the area of wage stabilization and relieved the company of the obligation to pay if profits were below the agreed-upon level. It is interesting to note that the base or payable level is approximately one-half of the profit level maintained during the war years beginning with 1940.

It was pointed out during negotiations that if its purpose was to increase production and efficiency, this plan as applied even under ideal conditions had little promise of success. Some efforts were directed toward the development of a graduated scale of bonus payment based on the profit level. These efforts, although looked upon favorably by several individual members of the company's official family, were finally vetoed by a majority as being unfeasible. Under the presently applied plan there is no incentive for the employees to do anything other than hope that a certain fixed minimum profit may accrue at the end of the fiscal year. They do not know from month to month whether they are maintaining a profit level sufficiently high to ensure the payment of the bonus. Even if they did know, there would be no incentive to increase the base minimum profit level. No relationship has been established between employee efforts and returns from the plan. If the company's profits are ten times greater than the base, the bonus share remains constant at 5 cents per hour. This plan is rightfully catalogued a failure.

This plan, however, should not be charged as a failure against profit sharing. It was neither conceived nor designed in any way to give the employees an opportunity to participate in a share of the profits of the company. It did not comprehend the development of a sense of partnership and participation in order to enhance profit-making possibilities. It was an instrument designed for the sole purpose of preventing the employees from joining a bona fide trade union. In this it failed, and the bonus payments remain a monumental evidence of this failure.

Profit-Sharing Plan Number 2

Case History no. 2	Failure
Company B	Steel fabricating
Employees	1800
1. Union affiliation	C.I.O.—first agreement in 1941
2. Type of labor agreement	Standard—maintenance of membership
3. Institution of profit-sharing plan	1941
4. Method of application	50 per cent of profit over 4 per cent of net worth
5. Method and time of payment	Percentage of total earnings for the year paid in a lump sum once each year.
6. Company's financial position	Good; earnings fair.

The employees of this company were organized in 1940. Early in 1941 the union won an N.L.R.B. election and was certified as a collective-bargaining agency. Negotiations with the company for a collective-bargaining agreement began in March of that year and dragged on through July without progress. The company had engaged the services of a well-known law firm to represent them in the negotiations. At no time did any of the company officials participate in the many conferences. The union pressed for a standard agreement; the corps of lawyers representing the company steadfastly refused to accept any of the existing clauses in the standard contract. Their patience exhausted because of the extended delay, the employees engaged in a work stoppage. They charged the company with refusal to bargain in good faith. The strike lasted for three weeks, during which time a great deal of ill will developed. It was settled when a memorandum of agreement covering the basic issues involved was signed, with a stipulation to the effect that the parties were to begin negotiations on the remaining differences within ten days after operations were resumed.

A meeting was scheduled for the seventh day after the strike was settled in order to complete the contract. The union's negotiating committee attending the meeting was surprised to find that the lawyers were conspicuously absent. Heretofore they had met exclusively with the company's attorneys; at this meeting they met for the first time with the company president, his assistant, and the plant manager.

The conference got under way and within three hours the remaining issues were disposed of in a satisfactory manner. The atmosphere was friendly and cooperative. At the conclusion of the meeting the company officials informed the union committee that they had decided it was to their best interests to do everything possible to get along with the union. The company president expressed the hope that a sound and friendly relationship might be developed. He frankly admitted that some of his friends in the industry and even his own board had been working on him. They had convinced him that his policy of fighting the union was extremely short-sighted. The union committee met this approach with mixed emotions. They were both pleasantly surprised and deeply suspicious.

Exactly four weeks after the strike settlement, the president of the company called the union committee to his office for a meeting. With a dramatic flourish he read a statement to them. The company had been giving much serious study to the many profit-sharing plans then in effect in American industry. They had now reached a decision. To cement a cooperative relationship with the union and as a gesture of good faith, they had developed a profit-sharing plan and were prepared to install it at once. He explained the details of the plan and its method of operation, so that they would be completely familiar, and so that the committee members could explain them to the union membership. The provisions were as follows:

A. In all good years the company had earned in excess of 4 per cent on its net worth.

B. Beginning with 1941 the employees would participate in a share of all profits above the 4 per cent net worth level.

C. Fifty per cent of all profits above this level of earnings would be placed in a pool for distribution to all employees.

D. Each employee would receive a proportionate share applied on a percentage basis to his total earnings during the preceding year's operations.

The sincerity of the management of the company in proposing the plan is undoubted. The wisdom of the move under the existing circumstances is questionable. The union had not even begun to function as such. Its officers had not the slightest idea of how the union affairs should be conducted. The newly elected grievance men had not as yet processed a grievance.

The bitterness and suspicion aroused during the organizational campaign and the subsequent strike were still fresh in the minds not only of the union membership but also of the supervisory force. The rank and file of the employees read into the announcement of the plan all sorts of trickery. They were not convinced that management had suffered a change of heart. "The company was using the plan as a technique to wreck the union. What was a profit anyway? Some wise guys could manipulate the books; every company had two sets anyway. The wage rates were too low. If the company was really honest about the whole business, it would use some of its profits to bring the low rates up. Let's go on a strike and make them give us the money now." These and similar remarks made the rounds of the mill. Although the local-union officers and committeemen were convinced that the plan had been offered in good faith, they were too inexperienced to present the case clearly. They did not know enough about their responsibilities, nor did they understand the plan well enough, to fight the tide of doubt and suspicion, so they rode along with the general opposition.

Reports of the reaction to the plan began seeping back to the president's office. He and his official family were first hurt, then angry and resentful. They were almost completely disillusioned. The president's plan had been misinterpreted and completely misunderstood. His immediate reaction was, "To hell with them and the whole damned business. I guess I've been a fool." The relationship with the union developed in a haphazard manner. No further efforts were exerted to make of the profit-sharing plan an instrument that would function properly.

In 1941 the employees received a bonus of 14 per cent; in 1942, 11 per cent; 1943, 9 per cent; in 1944, 12½ per cent; in 1945, 7½ per cent. Approximately $5,500,000 was paid out in the five-year period.

The situation today is just about the same as it was back in 1941. The same efficiency level has been maintained. As an incentive to induce greater teamwork and productive efficiency, the plan has failed. It has produced no tangible effect whatsoever and is now generally accepted as a part of the general wage structure. As a matter of course, when the share dropped to the 7½ per cent level in 1945, there was a great deal of griping. This plan can likewise be catalogued a failure.

This plan was never afforded an opportunity to succeed. It had at its inception one of the basic ingredients so necessary for success—sincerity of purpose. From this foundation, with care and effort, it might well have been developed into something extremely worth while. However, such consideration was woefully lacking. Confidence and a stable relationship, basic factors necessary for successful development, were conspicuously absent. The timing of the proposal was ill advised. Months of constant effort in order to allay suspicion and bitterness should have preceded the application of the plan. The simple device of announcing a plan developed on a unilateral basis, and then sitting back complacently awaiting results, has seldom achieved the desired objective. This plan not only failed as an instrument of profit sharing, but the impact of its initial reception has so disillusioned the management of this company that they have not recovered from the shock. Its failure haunts every collective-bargaining conference, every grievance meeting, and has made it virtually impossible to proceed in the orderly development of a stable, mutually beneficial, collective-bargaining relationship.

Profit-Sharing Plan Number 3

Case History no. 3	Success
Company C	Steel fabricating
Employees	125
1. Union affiliation	C.I.O.—first agreement in 1937

2. Type of labor agreement — Standard—union shop
3. Institution of profit-sharing plan — 1945
4. Method of application — 50 per cent of operating profits
5. Method and time of payment — Share applied by percentage basis on each month's profits to total earnings paid on eleventh day of each month.
6. Company's financial position — Good

The employees of this company were organized in 1937, and a satisfactory labor agreement was negotiated within a week following certification of the union as the bargaining agent by the N.L.R.B. The company was a leader in its particular segment of the fabricating industry. Its wage structure was the highest in the community and in the industry; and it had the reputation of being a consistently good profit maker.

The relationship between the union and the company had been a stable, healthy one. In nine years of collective bargaining there had not been a work stoppage of any description. In 1942 a labor-management production committee was set up, and it functioned with much success during the war period.

The labor-management production committee was composed of a subcommittee in each of the five operating departments. The union elected one representative to act on each of the subcommittees and management appointed a representative to serve in like capacity. Their function was to meet at least twice each month to discuss production problems in their particular department and to review all suggestions made by the employees of the department for improvements in productivity and efficiency.

The main committee, which was designated the production and planning committee, consisted of three management representatives—the company president, the general manager, and the auditor—and three union members—the local-union president and two members elected by the union membership. Meetings of the committee were held at least once each month, and minutes of the subcommittee meetings were reviewed. All controversial issues which developed in subcommittee meeting were disposed of by this main committee.

Well pleased with the results of their joint efforts to increase efficiency, and with a sincere desire to continue these efforts during the postwar period, a joint committee made up of management and union representatives began to examine the various types of profit-sharing plans in effect throughout American industry.

The committee's investigation of existing profit-sharing plans began in August 1944 and continued for several months. After a thorough study and a complete analysis of existing plans, they developed one which seemed to fit their particular needs. At this point the joint committee brought their recommendations to the international offices of the union for counsel and review. If the plan was approved, it was to be installed immediately.

Here the committee encountered a serious disappointment. They had developed a straight profit-sharing plan that was not approvable under wage stabilization rules. The problem of producing a temporary plan that would conform to War Labor Board restrictions was then assigned to the experts of the international union and the president of the company. After weeks of joint study, it was agreed to request N.W.L.B. approval of a plan using as a factor the ratio of labor costs to production values. This ratio had remained fairly constant during the 1938–1944 period. Its high point was 1 to 2.86 and its low point 1 to 2.69, with an average of 1 to 2.77. At this level the company's profit had averaged about 4 per cent on net worth. It had not operated in the red over a fourteen-year period. All employees except the president of the company participated in the plan on the basis of 1 per cent increase in earnings for each 1 per cent increase in efficiency whether they were on a salary or an hourly rate. The following table indicates the graduated levels of bonus payment at various ratio levels.

Sales Value of Production for Each Dollar of Labor Cost	Bonus: Percentage of Wages
2.77	0
2.80	1
2.83	2
2.85	3
2.88	4
2.91	5
3.05	10
3.19	15
3.32	20
3.46	25
3.60	30
3.74	35
3.88	40
4.02	45
4.16	50

In other words, the percentage of increase in earnings each pay, referred to as a bonus, was equal to the percentage of increase in the ratio of production value to labor cost over the 1944 ratio of 2.77. Had there been a change in the selling price of the items produced, in the cost of materials, or in any factor other than volume of production, a compensating change would have been made in the base on which this bonus was calculated.

The joint operating and administrative committee working with management was given an intensive course of education in the many important factors relating to the business. Controllable cost factors were stressed particularly, in order that all employees might get a clear idea of what they, as a group, could contribute in their efforts to increase productive efficiency. Fixed charges and the impact of greater productivity on unit costs were emphasized. Fuel, material, tools and supplies, delay factors, rejects, salvaged products, better and easier ways of getting the job done—all these and many more problems were tackled. The committee met almost nightly in an effort to make this information available to all employees and to get their suggestions. The problems that had been peculiar to management were now common problems.

A new and improved method of getting material into the shop was developed, reducing unloading cost by 20 per cent. Scrap losses were cut 11 per cent. A bottleneck between the shaping and welding department that had long been a source of expense and difficulty was quickly removed. The bosses were goaded into energetic activities in their efforts to keep ahead of the workers who had their first real opportunity to exercise their know-how and were bent on making good at it. Cost clerks, welders, engineers, and machinists, together with laborers and the plant manager, all had a common interest and were busily engaged as a group in improving that interest. The War Labor Board finally approved the plan. A review of the first nine months of its operation indicates clearly the results attained:

Monthly Ratio of Labor Cost and Production Value

January	1 to 3.56
February	1 to 2.95[1]
March	1 to 3.98
April	1 to 4.15
May	1 to 3.80
June	1 to 3.50
July	1 to 3.30
August	1 to 3.53
September	1 to 4.41

[1] Severe snowstorm halted transportation and prevented the men from getting to work.

The change in ratio over this nine-month period was an average of 1 to 3.70, compared with a base ratio in 1944 of 1 to 2.77.

At the end of the first year's operations under this plan, the company's profit was *two and one-half times greater* than it would have been had the 1 to 2.77 ratio prevailed, and each employee of the company had received a monthly share in the benefits of increased efficiency of approximately 41 per cent applied to his base wage rate or salary. At the end of the year, it was mutually decided to change this plan to a straight profit-sharing application. The reasons for the change were that both the union and management recognized factors inherent in the original application that might under certain conditions work a hardship on the company. If, for instance, the demand for the product did not permit full production schedules, the employees could maintain their bonus earnings, and, because of constant fixed charges, the company might well suffer losses. The workers' acceptance of this point was possible only because they understood in detail the whole financial picture.

Both parties realized that plant improvements or new equipment installed to improve operating efficiency might drastically affect the ratio of labor costs to sales value. If this situation did arise, it would necessitate a change in the factors in order to protect the company's interests. The local union itself initiated the action for a change to the profit-sharing plan. A series of comparisons tended to show that, had the employees shared in 50 per cent of the profits before taxes during 1945, they would have received approximately 37 per cent on their earnings, a few points below the 41 per cent share accomplished under the labor-cost production-value plan. Both the union and management agreed to replace the old plan with the new profit-sharing arrangement effective January 1, 1946. The provisions were:

A. Fifty per cent of the profits before taxes for each month would be paid out as a share on the twentieth day of the succeeding month.

B. The proportionate share figured percentagewise would be applied to the total earnings of each employee for the month in which the profit was earned.

The results achieved in 1946 under the profit-sharing plan were even better than those obtained in 1945. Even though there developed a time lag between a general wage increase in January of 19 cents per hour and an increase in sales price allowed by O.P.A., the employees' share in 1946 averaged out at 54 per cent and the company's profits, before taxes, almost doubled the 1945 figure.

The employees are kept constantly informed of their day-by-day progress. A huge clocklike instrument just inside the main factory entrance records the estimated levels of efficiency being maintained during the current month. One set of hands on the instrument shows the preceding month's levels as compared with the current month.

The results of this joint effort are best exemplified in an action taken by the production-committee members of the local union. On discovering that the plant manager, who was also the company president, did not participate on a salary basis but only in the profits, they voluntarily voted him a $12,000 a year salary, despite the fact that the contract covering the plan did not provide for any change whatsoever and this meant $12,000 less in profits for division.

It is important to note that when the Steelworkers' Union made their demand for an 18.5 cent increase per hour in January, 1946, causing the shutdown of practically all steel plants, this company was one of the few that maintained operations and applied the increase immediately. In fact the company president was more concerned about the application than were his employees. He reasoned that if they got it one way, they just would not get it the other, and it made little difference to him. He did refuse to deal in half cents, however, and for payroll simplification made it an even 19 cents.

It is pertinent to note that although there has been much controversy over the request of some unions to look at the books, the management of this company invites the union to do so. It was at management's insistence that the following clause was inserted in the profit-sharing agreement: "The United Steelworkers of America, C.I.O., shall have access to the books of the company at any time in order to verify the operating statements."

Two years have elapsed since this provision was placed in the original agreement, yet the union has at no time found it necessary to exercise these rights.

The most interesting factor concerning this plan is that the company is in a highly competitive segment of the steel-fabricating industry. Before adopting the plan, it had been considered the leader in its field. Its wage rates were the highest of nineteen companies surveyed, and since 1930 it had been a consistent profit maker. This marked degree of improvement in productive efficiency was achieved from a level which was considered, costwise to be almost perfect. There was no broad area of inefficiency and sloppy management to begin with.

All possible care was exercised in developing this successful plan. A stable union-management relationship predated its application. The plan itself was the product of joint efforts and understanding. A complete sense of partnership and participation was fully developed *before* the plan was put into operation. The end point was clear and concise. To ensure success, every possible effort was expended in outlining the contribution all employees could make. The workers today know just as much about the company's business as does the boss. They are in every practical sense partners in the venture. The president of the company has stated publicly that the success achieved by this plan would have been impossible without the organization of the employees in a bona fide labor union. He reasons that organized cooperation is most effective and that to get it he must have organized employees.

The Skeptic's Retort

Much has been written and reported concerning the successes that were achieved with union-management cooperation plans of the pre-war period. Studies reveal that practically all the plans were a product of expediency. Most companies and unions that engaged in such programs did so for selfish reasons. The companies involved were generally in a bad way financially, unable to meet competition, and were driven into this type of relationship in an effort to save themselves. Self-preservation and job security were the motivating forces.

Almost without exception, the experts who study profit sharing ask if this type of cooperation could be achieved between union and management in a firm that was operating successfully and making money. Case no. 3 (together with several others that have been developed in the past few years) answers this question satisfactorily. Now these same skeptics are again voicing fears and uncertainties. They are wondering what would happen if profits disappeared and a division was no longer possible. Between the two extremes there is a salient point that they have missed entirely. Whether it be a motivation fostered by a fear for job security or a desire for participation in the benefits of increased efficiency, if the fundamentals of participation and partnership are properly developed, the incentive to produce at the highest possible degree of efficiency is constant.

In any event, success can be achieved only if the employees, through their union, are taken into management's confidence. This is admittedly a broad statement; but let us consider its ramifications. What are the problems affecting the industry, the company, or the plan? The worker would like to know about them. He is anxious to contribute his know-how and intelligence in helping solve these problems. He is not, as a rule, the unthinking, selfish person many people would have us believe. He needs an outline and a proper sense of direction. Granted that a normal evolutionary development has taken him from the area of strife and suspicion, fighting for the very existence of his union, into the area of complete acceptance, a new and different set of constructive activities and responsibilities must replace those he has discarded.

If management expects to gain anything beneficial from these new relationships, it must now devote just as much time and effort in building with the union a complete sense of participation as it has probably spent in the past in fighting the union. As the industrial psychologist might put it, the egoistic needs of the group must be satisfied. Participation and partnership on a democratic basis will furnish these satisfactions.

In all successful plans, whether based on profit sharing or other acceptable factors of measurement, an outline of the future course of the business insofar as it is humanly foreseeable is a prime requisite. Departmental committees, meeting jointly with management, should be given all facts and figures on costs pertaining to their particular departmental operations. This information should deal especially with the costs that are controllable.

Committees should be rotated in order to reach the broadest possible degree of understanding and participation. Each union and management representative on these departmental committees should exercise good judgment in bringing into the meetings from time to time those employees of the department who have the greatest experience and knowledge of the problem outlined for discussion.

The unionization of the workers in many industries in the past ten years must necessarily bring a new approach to this type of problem. Whether or not a union is involved, if profit-sharing plans are to be successful, they must be a product of joint formulation, participation, and responsibility.

Controllable Cost Factors

There has been too much mystery and secrecy in connection with cost factors. The old shibboleth that they cannot be divulged because of competition has broken down. The overemphasis placed on labor costs, inherent in most of the presently applied wage incentive plans, is due for some modification.

The Bureau of Census in its 1939 Census of Manufactures covering all manufacturing industries showed that the total wage bill in these industries averaged 16 per cent of the plant sales dollar. This figure has undergone some alterations during the war years but it seems unlikely that it has increased above the 20 per cent level. The fact remains that close to 80 per cent of the sales dollar is expended in areas outside the wage bill. There is every indication that in the average plant and industry there necessarily must exist a wide range of costs that lend themselves to worker control. In a general way these factors may seem somewhat broad and indefinite. They will probably include material costs, fuel, power, and general overhead (administrative and factory). Broken down by departments they become more tangible and understandable. Here they may be translated into many subdivided areas of control, such as tools and supplies; fuel consumed; materials wasted; yields, scrap per cent or quality control; impact of greater efficiency on burden costs; delay factors of all descriptions; and impact on costs of processing defective materials.

Few open-hearth workers were aware of the fact that fuel costs per ton were greater than labor costs, that each 1 per cent increase in yields, or the percentage of what came out over what went in, meant a saving of 25 cents per ton; that each hour a furnace was down there was a $45 loss, and that fixed charges were $10 per ton at a certain level of production and could be cut almost in half at double that level.

Few men employed in a rolling mill knew that each hour the mill was down represented a $600 loss. Machine delays and crane delays are costly and represent lowered efficiency. Few employees in a heater plant knew that the burden placed on a heater that sold for $45 was $16.50 when the production level was at 125 units in an eight-hour turn. When they thoroughly understood the impact, not just on labor costs but also on fixed charges, and participated in the over-all benefits, they discovered ways of increasing production to the 200-unit level. When they discovered how costly it was for a defective product to be sent out to the customer and returned, or to require servicing at a far-distant point, they, as a group, exercised much more control over this problem. When they found that a product that was definitely defective in the second operation often went on through fifteen more operations before being scrapped, they had a full knowledge of how costly it was, and reduced this practice to an unbelievable minimum.

Management knows best just what its controllable cost factors are. If a profit-sharing plan is to work successfully, the employees who participate and make it work must have an outline. If they are forced to struggle, with no sense of direction and without a full knowledge of what they can contribute, no worth-while results need be expected.

All suggestions designed to increase efficiency should be carefully screened, so that every ounce of know-how available in the working force may be utilized to the best advantage. If this fundamental program is carried out, there should be little need for the fear that is most generally expressed in the question: "What will happen when profits are no longer available to distribute?" If the working force is aware through detailed knowledge of the whole situation that there are no profits for distribution because the company is operating in the red, then they will have a powerful incentive to accomplish the job more efficiently. This background of understanding is most essential to a successful profit-sharing plan.

At about the time when the unions made their last general wage increase demands, there was an influx of proposals from companies suggesting the joint application of various types of profit-sharing plans. In most instances, the unions were forced to reply: "Too little, too late." The time to propose a profit-sharing plan is after the wage increase is granted. It cannot function as a substitute. In a recent example of this approach, typical of many, the president of a fairly large company visited the union office to discuss a plan he had developed. After some exploratory conversation, he outlined his proposal:

A. He did not want to grant a wage increase.

B. His company had never earned over 4 per cent on invested capital.

C. He would divide with his employees 20 per cent of all profits over 6 per cent on invested capital.

Naturally the union was not interested in either the timing or the provisions offered.

Profits, to the average worker, have little significance. The term at best has an unsavory history, one of vague conceptions, subject to all sorts of manipulations by so-called mumbo-jumbo experts. Quite naturally, the worker associates the term with his past experiences. He remembers too well that every time he asked for a wage increase, he discovered to his surprise that the company was losing money. If, in his ignorance, he expressed some disbelief and a lack of understanding, an auditor and an accountant were called in to prove to him that the company was broke.

Conclusion

The analysis of these plans indicates that a sense of participation and partnership is the fundamental prerequisite. If this is fully developed, the type of plan itself is of secondary importance. The employees must be given an opportunity to exercise some degree of control over job security. Their efforts directed toward greater efficiency and productivity must be clearly and directly related to returns. With this foundation the employees of Company C continued to expand and improve their cooperation and efficiency levels even though the method of reward was changed. The substitution of the profit-sharing plan for the one using labor cost ratio to sales value of production in no way influenced the broad over-all results. Hundreds of companies, particularly the smaller ones, caught in the vise of increasingly difficult competition, are looking with greater favor on profit-sharing plans as an answer to their problem. If they are prepared to spend all the time, effort and care necessary for the constructive development of such a plan, they may find their answer. If not, they would be well advised to steer completely clear of the idea of profit sharing.

FREDERICK G. LESIEUR

APPENDIX C..

Local Union Experience
with a Cooperation Plan

The title of this paper could just as well be "The Growth of a Local Union with a Cooperation Plan." That is just what has taken place with Local Union No. 3536 of the United Steelworkers of America at the Lapointe Machine Tool Company during the past four years.

In 1945, a majority of employees of the Lapointe Machine Tool Company sought to organize and won an election for a union and became Local Union No. 3536 of the United Steelworkers of America. The election was won by a fairly close vote. Management of the company resisted our attempts to associate together in a union. We retaliated by fighting back. There existed a great deal of mutual distrust. The fact of the matter is, we not only distrusted management but, in many instances, each other.

When the steel industry went out on strike in 1946 for 18½ cents an hour, we also went out on strike. Our strike was a long, bitter one in which the company after being closed down for nine weeks

Reprinted by permission from the *Proceedings of the Fourth Annual Meeting of the Industrial Relations Research Association*, 1951.

won an injunction over us and we lost our legal right to strike.
Nevertheless, we did not go back to work but we were finally forced
to settle not for 18½ cents per hour but for 15 cents for day workers
and 10 cents for piece workers. Neither side really won as the company lost a lot of money and also good customers, and the union did
not get all it was asking for. During the negotiations for the settlement of the strike the company said that when we were back to work
they would welcome any ideas from the union that might help
production and bring about a better relationship between the union
and the company. At that time I don't believe anyone ever gave this
a second thought.

Later on that year one of the union members read an article in *Life*
magazine which was entitled, "Every Man a Capitalist." This was a
story about another concern in eastern Ohio which had installed a plan
designed to establish harmonious and cooperative union-management
relations. This plant was also represented by the Steelworkers'
Union. He gave the article to our Union President, Jack Ali, who
felt after reading the article that many of the ills that this other
plant formerly had we also had at the present time. The executive
board of the union discussed this article with the membership at the
next union meeting and also contacted our international to try to find
out just what was going on at this other concern.

Fortunately for us, we discovered that Mr. Joseph N. Scanlon,
Director of the Research Department of the Steelworkers' International Union, had installed this plan at this particular company, and
was now on leave of absence from the Steelworkers' Union and on
the faculty of the Massachusetts Institute of Technology. This was
only twenty-five mlies from our plant. Our local union committee
with Roy Stevens of the international union went down to M.I.T.
and had a meeting with Mr. Scanlon to discuss the possibilities of
applying the so-called Scanlon Plan to our plant. The Committee left
M.I.T. quite impressed with what they had heard about real participation and not somebody trying to give a group of people a so-called
sense of participation.

The next step was, just how could we get the company interested.
Our president, Jack Ali, aproached Mr. Edward Dowd, Vice President and General Manager of the company. His first reaction was
that there were thousands of schemes and plans throughout the country, and all that he could discover from surveys that he had made
was that they stimulated interest and then gradually died out. Jack
Ali prevailed on him to at least meet Mr. Scanlon and discuss the Plan
with him. Dowd finally agreed, and the meeting was arranged. After

a careful investigation by both the union and the company, including a visit to the Ohio plant, it was finally decided to try to apply the Plan to our operations.

The Situation before the Plan Went into Effect

There were many obstacles that had to be ironed out before we could even think of participation. Management had installed a piece-work system which predated unionization by many years. Its use had encouraged competition among the employees and had left little room for teamwork. Through its operation some workers personally profited. Many others were left in what seemed to them to be in the category of half citizens or forgotten people. It operated in such a manner that each employee had to think only of himself and the devil could take the hindmost. There existed some bitter feelings among the employees.

Not many of us cared particularly about the quality of our work. Not many of us were interested in the quality of the machines and equipment we were building or for that matter in the success of the enterprise. This was management's responsibility, and rightly or wrongly we had generally concluded that they didn't believe it was any of our damn business. Certainly this had some effect upon the quality of our products.

Our only meetings or contacts with management were on conflicting issues concerning grievances and wage differences. Usually, management would not give an inch and neither would we if we could help it.

Management quite often was unable to make shipments and deliveries on promised schedules. Many customers turned elsewhere for similar equipment. As business went elsewhere, employment diminished. We all felt insecure and uncertain. In short, everyone including the management was losing. The union officers realized this state of affairs could not continue indefinitely.

Putting the Plan into Effect

With the help of Mr. Scanlon we finally reached an understanding. The company management promised not to interfere with the union. As members of the union we promised to work with management. It is important to remember that cooperation is a two-way street. Neither party can do all the cooperating.

A joint committee was set up to make a study of the payroll and

cost records over a period of several years that represented periods of
prosperity and depression. From this study a measurement was devised that showed clearly the ratio of labor costs to the sales value
of the finished end product.

It was agreed that to whatever extent production could be increased without increased labor costs, the difference in value of output would be returned to the employees each month as a percentage
of their hourly rates of pay. To state it another way, for every 1 per
cent of increased output per month above the norm established as a
result of the study, the employees would receive 1 per cent added to
their regular wages. The incentive or piecework system that had
previously pitted each man against his fellow worker was abolished.
New hourly wage rates were established by mutual agreement that
represented the average piecework earnings for an agreed-upon prior
period.

Mr. Scanlon worked out a memorandum of understanding jointly
with the company and the union. These were the rules that we would
go by. In no way could this memorandum conflict with our labor
agreement with the company.

The plant was divided into seven departments: office, engineering
and five others out in the factory, for the purpose of setting up production committees. The employees in each department elected a
production committeeman to represent them on the committee. The
departmental foreman or supervisor was designated by the management as their representative on the committee. These committees
would meet individually in each department at least twice a month or
more often, if necessary. They would discuss suggestions or proposals
brought in by the employee member of the committee and if acceptable to the foreman or supervisor, and within the jurisdiction of the
department, be placed into effect. A record was made of all suggestions which were taken up at this meeting, whether they were put
into effect, whether there was a difference of opinion, or whether
it was a suggestion that might involve another department. Each production committeeman had the right to bring in one or two employees
into this meeting with him. This was to broaden the participation
and also allow anyone who had made a suggestion to come in and
present it himself. Also taken up at this meeting were production
problems, scheduled in advance if possible, that confront the department. All suggestions or proposals would then be forwarded to a
top committee called the screening committee.

The screening committee was composed of the top officials of the company and a like number elected by the union. Their duties were first to go over the results of the previous month and announce the bonus. Then go over the possibilities of the present month. Next they would go over all the minutes from the production-committee meetings held in that previous month and act on all suggestions or proposals that were not acted upon at the production-committee level. They would also review those proposals or suggestions that were placed in effect at the production committee level. This committee was considered more or less a court of higher appeal where suggestions would be acted upon on a merit basis and personalities would not be involved. This committee would also discuss the possibilities of future business and the problems we were having with our equipment out in the field. A careful record of all suggestions would be kept. The final decision as to the practicability and the usefulness of each suggestion rested with management.

The employees were duly informed as these plans developed. They were urged to discuss freely with their departmental committeeman any ideas or proposals designed to eliminate waste, improve methods of operation and increase output. Employees were not to be individually rewarded for those of their suggestions which were adopted and made use of. The fact is, they do not want individual or personal rewards. That causes rivalry and ill will. By putting the increased share of the increased output into a pool or common fund and distributing it monthly as a percentage of their hourly rates, all share equitably. Maturity, stability and a healthy regard for each other are the by-products.

Results

Since the Scanlon Plan, as our present set-up is called, was established over four years ago, 1050 suggestions have been submitted by approximately 300 employees; 905 have been accepted and put into effect by management; 51 are awaiting further action, while 94 have been rejected.

The net effect of this cooperative effort has been to increase production and lower costs. The extent of this is reflected in the bonus percentage added to the hourly rates of pay. This has ranged from a low of 1 per cent to a high of 37 per cent. The average for this year has been aproximately 17 per cent.

During the past four years the Lapointe Machine Tool Company has undergone just about every phase that any business in this country will undergo. There were periods of a great deal of work, other periods when work wasn't so plentiful; there were layoffs, and then the present emergency with the plant doubling and then tripling its size. The management states that, while we doubled and tripled our size, the employees were trained in new jobs in one-third the time it formerly took.

Now here is what has happened to the union during this period of time. When the Plan was installed in 1947, the bargaining unit consisted mainly of the factory and engineering. We did not have a union shop and approximately 60 per cent of the people in the bargaining unit belonged to the union. And then in 1949 when the union negotiated a union shop agreement, there were only three people who were eligible to join the union who did not belong. The bargaining unit had grown from the engineering and shop to include the office group.

Formerly, we used to handle around 10 to 15 written grievances a month. During the past four years there have been only five written grievances, all being settled before going to arbitration. Now this doesn't mean that there aren't problems and that the union is not doing its job. We credit this change in conditions mainly to the fact that, when a problem does arise, both sides want a fair and equitable settlement. Also we believe the company looks at the facts on our side more, and we also take a look at their point of view perhaps a little more than we formerly did.

As far as union meetings are concerned, they are now well attended. The reason for this, we feel, is that now, rather than getting together each month and discussing only grievances and negotiations, a whole new area of discussion has been opened to the union. This new area involves discussion on the problems of conducting a business, production problems, suggestions, outlook for future business and the action taken on these problems.

There are many things that have come about under participation that we don't believe we would ever have had any other way. The financial benefits derived from the Plan, even though they have been good, are not the most important factors. People now at Lapointe think of each other a little more than they ever did and try to help each other, realizing that when they do everyone benefits—the younger people helping the older workers and the older workers showing some of their tricks and skills of long experience to the younger workers. The result has been an increase in the solidarity and strength of the local union.

Meeting Problems as They Came Along

Here are a few of the many incidents which tend to show the type of relationship that we enjoy.

When we first adopted the Plan, the company felt we had a large enough backlog of orders to carry us through any amount of increase in productivity that they thought possible. At the end of three months, the company could readily see that this backlog was nowhere large enough. A meeting was called between the union and the company to discuss this problem. The company announced that Mr. Prindiville, the Company President, and Ed Dowd, the Vice President, were going out on the road to see what they could do about bringing more business in. During the discussions, it was discovered that even if they were able to get more business in immediately, it would take from four to six weeks to get it out of engineering. So we were faced with the problem of not having enough work for the people in the factory. It was decided to carry these people on, and this number amounted to between 50 and 60 workers, until there was enough work for everyone. But the union and the company fully understood that there could not be any bonuses earned during this period of time. When new orders began to come in, we were approaching our vacation time. We were all amazed to find that engineering offered to forego its vacation until a later date and work while the factory was shut down to expedite the orders out into the factory. This surprised us workers out in the factory as there was always a constant bickering between the factory and engineering on production problems prior to the Plan. We even began to think that maybe the engineers were also human.

Later on, we discovered the reason why one of our grinding departments was continually running low on work. We were not able to compete against other broach companies. This problem was taken up with the workers in the department involved, and the union asked the company to set their prices at a competitive level in order to bring work in. The company was a little reluctant to do so as they showed us some of the large losses which this department had taken. Nevertheless, we still maintained that if the company would go out and get some of this business, we would do all that we could to make it a profitable job. Finally, the company agreed to take another order for these tools and had to bid $17 each below our former manufacturing cost. The order was for 1000 broaches. All workers concerned with this job got together and came forth with their ideas on how the job should be run. Consequently, on the first 100, there was only a slight loss. The remaining 900 were made with a profit of better than 10 per cent.

There became a much closer working harmony between night and day shifts. Workers were no longer adverse to carrying on with jobs from another shift. Instead of each worker hiding his pet jigs or tools at the end of a shift, these tools were willingly shared.

Another incident which showed us just what we could do if we had the facts to work with occurred when the company discussed the business for the present month at one of our screening committee meetings. They indicated that due to product mix, also a low volume of work on the machine floor, it would be impossible to make a bonus let alone not have a large deficit. We all became conscious of this and got together to see what we could do with this bad month. No one had any thought in mind of making a bonus but the emphasis was just to try to break even. When the month was finished, and the figures compiled, we discovered that we had earned a 2½ per cent bonus. As this was announced throughout the factory, the workers seemed much happier than the month they had earned a 37 per cent bonus. This was due to the fact that they felt they had accomplished the impossible.

Conclusion

We believe at Lapointe that this new way of life is the only way, and we would never want to go back to where we were. Our union agreement with the company provides for average hourly rates of pay that are equal to, if not higher than, those made by any other company in the machine tool industry. Our contract contains all the standard provisions with respect to wages, hours, and working conditions. We have a union shop without any strings attached, also a pension plan. Our take-home pay is probably the highest in the industry. During the past four years, the Plan has never interfered with collective bargaining. In fact, if anything, it has helped it.

The company has similarly benefited from this program. The ability to turn out a high-quality product and make deliveries on time has enabled the company to build up its prestige. Lost customers have been regained and new ones acquired. All because we have learned, the hard way it is true, how to work together as self-respecting and equal participants in a common endeavor from which we all earn our livelihood. We believe as a result of our own experience over a period of four years that similar results can be had in almost any manufacturing plant. Neither the Scanlon Plan or any other scheme to increase productivity will work unless there is the will and the determination on the part of both management and labor to make it work. This is not possible unless there is good faith, mutual respect, and confidence in the hearts of all the participants.

ROBERT C. TAIT

APPENDIX D . .

Some Experiences with
a Union-Management
Cooperation Plan

I was living in relative tranquility as Vice President of the Mellon
Bank in Pittsburgh when I was approached by the board of directors
of Stromberg-Carlson Company and asked to accept the presidency.
The then President and Chairman were both retiring simultaneously
as of April 1, 1949. I was a native of Rochester, had been born and
raised there and therefore already knew a good deal about Stromberg-
Carlson Company and some of its problems. It presented a real challenge, and after some study and investigation I accepted the board's
offer. May I hasten to add that I was not asked to come back to
Rochester as a banker to head Stromberg-Carlson Company. The
Mellon Bank had never had any relationships with the company, and
what the company needed was not banking experience so much as
sound business direction and improved industrial relations. It was
an old company, established in 1894, that had survived some pretty

Reprinted from the *Proceedings of the Fourth Annual Meeting of the Industrial
Relations Research Association*, 1951, by permission of the author and the publisher.

rough weather in the past, had established a fine reputation for quality, but had of late years seemed to slow down.

The company had a local independent union known as Rochester Independent Workers Local No. 1, and almost immediately after my arrival on the scene negotiations with respect to a new labor contract began. Not having yet had time to know even who was who, I let the incumbent head of industrial relations conduct negotiations in the traditional manner and pretty much kept my hand out of it—that is, until it appeared that the negotiations were getting nowhere and the union was insisting on a pretty substantial wage increase. The company was losing money, and because of a number of circumstances it appeared certain that it would lose money for the entire year of 1949. The sieve was leaking in all directions at once. The company had not yet gotten into the television business with its own designs; the radio business had suddenly fallen apart, and it had had to discontinue in February a substantial production authorization that had to be completed some time or face a loss of several hundred thousand dollars; development work in our XY switch, which is the heart of our automatic dial telephone system, had not yet been completed; the sound equipment business only amounted to about a million dollars; and the very successful broadcasting division with a 50,000 watt clear channel AM station, which had been a steady earner for many years, was plunging into TV the middle of June that year and facing operating losses for an indefinite and unknown period in the future.

A wage increase under these conditions would appear suicidal, so I asked the Union Negotiating Committee if I could appear before them personally, and did so. I told them what the company was facing quite frankly and specifically, and made pretty much of a personal appeal for six months grace under the present contract to give me a chance to try to get the company back on its feet. They said they would buy my appeal if I could sell it to the people, but that negotiations had proceeded so far and so long that they didn't feel they could sell this themselves; in other words, I should call a general meeting of the employees and merely tell them that I had asked the Union Negotiating Committee for permission to appeal directly to them, and not say anything about the committee's willingness to grant the appeal. As a result we had a general meeting of all the employees that could jam into our cafeteria on a hot day in June. Temperature outside was over 90 and it must have been 110 in that room, but to make a long story short the people in the plant voted to grant my request and not only extend the contract for six months but for a year.

I bore you with all of this in order to lead up to the point that, among other things in making my appeal to our employees, I said that I was interested in profit sharing as such but recognized fully the many pitfalls in the way of a successful profit-sharing plan and the fact that perhaps two profit-sharing plans fail for every one that actually becomes successful; that I would in the ensuing months conduct a study of our company's peculiarities in an effort to come up with some form of workable profit-sharing plan; that they must not consider this a commitment to adopt any plan but merely to study the possibilities.

Introduction of the Scanlon Plan

Sometime during the Christmas holidays that year I ran across and happened to read the *Fortune* article on the Scanlon Plan that appeared in the January 1950 issue. I had never heard of Joe Scanlon before, but the thing that jumped out of the page as I started to read the article was the name of the first company that had adopted a Scanlon Plan. It was the Adamson Company in East Palestine, Ohio, and I happened to know that company well. As a loaning officer of the Mellon Bank I had assisted young Don Gillis in his purchase of the company from Adamson, and in connection with our financing I of course had had access to all of his operating figures over a period of some two years. Adamson Company had gone from a productivity ratio of measurement to a straight profit-sharing plan, under which the company cut profit before taxes at the end of each month right in half, one-half going to employees and the balance to management, and out of the latter of course came income taxes. I used to take the Adamson figures into our loan committee meetings at the Mellon Bank just to show the boys what a smart little company could do. Its wage bonuses were astounding, especially when you consider that Adamson was probably the lowest cost operator in their line of business. I thus knew their profit-sharing plan intimately—but I never knew it had been inspired by Joe Scanlon.

Well, anyhow I decided to try to get to know Joe Scanlon. I called him here at M.I.T. and made an appointment and jumped on a plane. My first talk with Joe was very interesting, because instead of my sizing him up, I quickly became aware of the fact that I was being screened, not he. In other words, he and his associates were digging down into my thinking to see what kind of a guy I was, and what kind of philosophy I held in respect to industrial relations in general. I guess I passed because Joe came over to Rochester shortly thereafter to make a preliminary examination of our company. After completion of this he decided to go ahead, and for the next several months he and we worked rather feverishly making studies in preparation for adoption by July 1st of a Scanlon Plan based on a measurement of productivity. We submitted the matter to vote of the entire plant, and approximately 90 per cent voted to adopt the Plan. As a matter of fact, the 10 per cent that opposed it I think were the people who might conceivably find their jobs no longer necessary under the Plan. Up until this time we had operated under a modified form of Bedaux system that appeared to have outworn its usefulness. The standards were loose, base rates were way below actual rates of pay, in many departments the incentive was gone entirely because the guaranteed rates far exceeded the minimum Bedaux rates, some workers had work banks of a month to six weeks, etc., etc.

We also had a suggestion system of the common type that appeared to have gotten not only into a rut but into something closely approximating a racket. An inside clique, some of whom were on the suggestion committee that evaluated awards, were consistently pulling down substantial awards, many of which seemed to be out of line with the benefits the company would derive. There were a good many instances where foremen, instead of making some improvement that was a part of their job, would tip a worker off to make such a suggestion and split the award if he got one. So we also had to throw out the suggestion system and try to encourage our people to make suggestions under the Scanlon Plan for the benefit of everyone rather than for the individual alone, in the realization, of course, that any suggestion that would reduce costs would be reflected in an increased bonus for all.

One of the first things we had done after my assumption of the presidency was to cut the company into vertical operating divisions. It had formerly been a horizontal organization with a manufacturing division, engineering division, sales division, etc. with "Iron Curtains" in between them. Only the broadcasting division operated as a separate vertical unit. We cut the manufacturing operations into three vertical divisions—radio-television, telephone, and sound equipment, each with its own engineering, sales force, etc. under a divisional general manager—not only in order to achieve better direction and control of operations but in order to uncover our strengths and weaknesses. Prior to this we couldn't even tell how much we made or lost in the radio business, telephone, sound equipment, or even broadcasting.

This divisional form of operation required a different form of production and screening committees under the Scanlon Plan than was customary practice. We set up production committees in each department of each division, composed of one representative from the work force and one from management. Then, because of our size and the diversity of products and related problems, we organized a screening committee composed of the general manager of that division and some of his top men, with an equal number of representatives from the work force. Minutes from the production committees of each division, with suggestions for savings or improved methods or performance, pass on to the divisional screening committees, which in turn screen out and either put into effect, refer for further study, or reject suggestions that have not been completed at the departmental level. The divisional screening committees in turn refer any suggestions that involve policy matters, financial appropriations outside the divisional budget, or any matters that overlap other divisions, to an over-all top committee called the planning and review committee. This committee is composed of the general managers of each of the manufacturing divisions, the heads of the finance and public and industrial relations divisions and myself, together with a like number of representatives of the union. This planning and review committee goes over the minutes of the divisional screening committees and performs the same function with respect to matters referred to it that the divisional screening committees perform for each division, in addition to which it tries to evaluate the strengths and weaknesses of our production and divisional screening committees in order to improve our lines of communication and stimulate activity where we seem to be falling down. This top planning and review committee further studies and jointly reviews the results of each month's operations as revealed by the figures in the calculation of the monthly bonus, if any, before it is officially announced to the employees.

This very roughly gives you an idea of the organizational structure of the committees that constitute our most important lines of communication. We have 48 production committees in the different departments of the three manufacturing divisions, plus the three divisional screening committees and the planning and review committees that I have just described. Thus our lines of communication go from a job in a department to the production committee for that department up to the divisional screening committee and from there, if necessary, to the planning and review committee.

As for suggestions, it is interesting to note that we have processed some 1300 suggestions, of which more than half have been approved and put into effect. About 30 per cent have been rejected because they were unfeasible or impractical, or in one way or another involved other considerations that more than outweighed the good, or an unwarranted cost in respect to the savings that might be expected. And about 20 per cent of the suggestions are still pending because they are of a nature that have to be worked out over a longer period of time before they can be put into effect or discarded.

Results

In the first six months of our operations under the Scanlon Plan, beginning July 1, 1950, we managed to earn a bonus every month that averaged approximately 12 per cent of our participating payroll over the six months period. Incidentally, everyone in the plant who is eligible participates under the Plan, including myself. I offered to stay out and offered to keep our top group of officers out of participation in the Plan, but after due consideration it was the consensus of the various committees that worked out the details of the Plan before its adoption that all of us should participate in respect to our base pay, on the theory that everyone should be able to contribute over a period of time in proportion to the pay he receives for his job. We pulled ourselves up rapidly in the latter months of 1950 to make a pretty fair earning year for the company as a whole.

This past year of 1951 confronted us with an entirely new set of problems. The telephone, sound equipment, and broadcasting divisions went on to greater volumes and profits than they had ever enjoyed before, but the bottom fell right out of the television market last spring, and it hasn't recovered yet. We were forced to shut down the lines in that division in April and couldn't start them up again until after the vacation period in July. Thus they were closed down for three full months, and the licking that division took financially during that period made it impossible for us to make enough in the other manufacturing divisions to earn a bonus. This was a very trying experience, because many people felt they were doing their jobs, their division was all right and there was no reason why they shouldn't get a bonus. We have had to educate them gradually, however, to the realization that the welfare of the company as a whole must be the underlying basis of our individual welfare. It has been a nice little lesson in the give and take that must exist for the welfare of the group as a whole, for it is perfectly obvious that management would be in a very tenuous position if stockholders found it paying out substantial wage bonuses and not making any money for the company.

This has undoubtedly been our most difficult problem to date—that is, the problem of education in the recognition of the over-all welfare of the company as the goal. This involves something beyond the control of any one individual. A man may improve his own productivity but have no control whatsoever over whether that produces better over-all results for the company, for some other man or department or division may be wasting or losing more than enough to offset his increased productivity. This, of course, is a fundamental problem in any group-sharing of the results of increased productivity or, for that matter, profit sharing itself. As you well know, it is frequently argued that profit sharing is unsound because the individual worker cannot control profits. One management decision, in respect, let's say, to inventories, may double or wipe out a company's profits for a particular period. On the other hand, we all know that profit sharing does work when properly conceived under proper leadership; for over a period of time management's major decisions affecting profits must maintain a good average or the management itself is no good, in which case no plan will work satisfactorily for the welfare of either the company or its employees.

Prospects and Conclusion

We now face another difficult challenge—which is the fair and proper measurement of productivity during a period of continually changing product mix as the result of the gradual shift from civilian to defense production. By the end of this coming year approximately half of our total dollar billing should be in defense work. Now it is less than 10 per cent. We cannot change our ratio of payroll cost to sales-value-added-by-manufacture—which is the fundamental measurement in our case—every month, and yet all of us know that any substantial shift in product mix affects that measurement, as does any substantial increase or decrease in over-all volume of production. It is our hope that the increased volume of production will more than offset any adverse effect that the changing percentages of civilian and defense work may have on the productivity ratio, at least until such time as we begin to level off at some relatively stable combination of civilian and defense production. Meantime we will be restudying our productivity computations and may alter the ratio once or several times, or for that matter, the entire basis of measurement.

As a matter of fact, it is in this flexibility and the meeting and solving of new problems together that I believe lies the ultimate success or failure of our Scanlon Plan. Admittedly we are a more complex industry than most of those that have adopted and are successfully

operating a Scanlon Plan.   Also a part of our business is highly
seasonal and cyclical.   On the other hand, I find no one who wants to
go back to our former modified Bedaux System of strictly individual
incentive, and I believe there is a growing recognition throughout our
plant of the need to, and determination to, cut and fit under changing
conditions until we find what works best for us.   This, to me, is the
fascinating part of our industrial relationships under our Scanlon Plan.

Index

171

www.ingramcontent.com/pod-product-compliance
Lightning Source LLC
Chambersburg PA
CBHW061311220326
41599CB00026B/4830